EVIDENCE OF

ANIMAL AFTERLIFE

Revised Edition

Edward Anderson, PhD

DEDICATION

To Anna and Boomer

Acknowledgements

I had plenty of help along the way, from people and animals. I need to express my special gratitude to the authors from whose work I draw here. Without their work, there would be no evidence for me to summarize. I have shared only a small portion of what they documented. I encourage you to read their books for yourself; sources are cited in each chapter.

I am also grateful to all the animals I have known. They have made my life better in countless ways.

Note on the Revised Edition

Initially, I planned on just fixing typos and rearranging some of the furniture, but as I got into it, I found myself rewriting major sections of the book. I also removed several parts that, in retrospect, I feel did not work well. In addition, I added proper footnotes and generally cleaned things up. Undoubtedly, I have created some new typos in the process, but such are the perils of self-publishing. Still, I think the book is better overall. I hope you enjoy it.

Table of Contents

Chapter 1

Introduction

The bond between humans and animals can be just as deep and profound as the link between humans. And the death of an animal companion can be just as painful as losing a human, sometimes more. When our animal friends die, we grieve. And we wonder, "Is that the end? Is the memory all that remains?"

Your answer to that question will shape how you experience the loss of your animal friend – whether the loss feels partial or total, time-limited or final. Your answer will shape more than just grief. It will affect how you see animals and how you relate to them.

Is there an afterlife? And if there is, do animals "get in," or just people? I hope this book will shed some light on those questions.

Why Am I Writing This Book?

My purpose is to summarize the published material on animal afterlife. I am writing primarily for people who wonder whether animals survive death in some non-physical form. Perhaps the person has lost a pet, or perhaps they anticipate that loss in the near future. Or perhaps they are just curious about the subject.

I will be drawing from the afterlife literature. By "afterlife literature," I mean books written by either professionals and laymen on topics such as near-death experiences, after-death communications, evidential mediumship, and the other areas you see listed in the Table of Contents. If you are skeptical about such topics, I understand. I have been reading the afterlife literature for about 20 years, and although it contains a fair amount of hokum, I'm convinced that, taken as a whole, it provides persuasive evidence of an afterlife – not the heaven and hell in the conventional sense, but an afterlife of some sort. You are certainly entitled to your skepticism, though. I'm a skeptical person myself. Healthy skepticism is a good thing (closed-minded skepticism is not, but that's another subject).

Unfortunately, most people are not acquainted with either the afterlife literature generally or with the small subset of that literature related to animal survival. Most people do not read the afterlife literature at all. Even if they do, they are not likely to encounter much material about animals, because most of that literature is focused on human beings. After all, human beings are the ones having the experiences, doing the investigations, and writing the books – so naturally, the focus is on human survival. Animals are an afterthought at best. Most of the time, they aren't even mentioned.

The material on animals is scattered around piecemeal, often buried in obscure places. Unless you read a lot of this material, you aren't going to know about it. Since I am in the position to know about it, I wanted to summarize it for other people, so that they didn't have to go digging themselves.

I gathered all the animal afterlife reports I could find, then categorized and classified them according to type. I will present that material to you in an easy-to-digest summary form.

I will just be presenting an overview, not an exhaustive survey. I will be skimming the surface, not plumbing the depths. It would be unethical of me to elaborate all the details, because I am drawing from others' work. I will relay some of the accounts, but just a small sample. I encourage you to read the original sources for more. There is a wealth of data I did not include. Sources are cited in each chapter, with the full list in the Bibliography.

In addition to summarizing evidence, I also want to make some arguments. I think it's important to have evidence and arguments for your beliefs – both can be persuasive in their own way. Although I will focus mostly on evidence, I will also intersperse a few arguments.

Overall, I intend the book for people who have lost a pet or anticipate that loss. I hope that seeing some evidence of animal afterlife, and hearing some of the arguments, will bolster your faith that your friend lives on in some form, and that you will see them again.

What Do I Mean by "Evidence"?

When I say "evidence," I do not mean evidence from controlled scientific experiments, published in peer-reviewed journals. Well, I do mean that, but that is not *all* I mean. Controlled scientific experiments published in peer-reviewed journals are one form of evidence – and a good one, to be sure – but they are not the only form of evidence. We live in a culture that idolizes science, so this may need some clarification.

There are many different forms of evidence, not just controlled scientific experiments. For example, careful observation is evidence (in fact, it is the foundation of good scientific investigation). Personal experience is also evidence. Without consulting personal experience, many sciences (e.g., medicine or any of the social sciences) would not have made much progress. Eye-witness accounts are also evidence. It is used every day in the courts.

When I use the word "evidence," then, that is mostly what I am referring to – observational data, personal experience, and eyewitness accounts.

Is that sort of evidence equivalent to controlled scientific experiments published in peer-reviewed journals? Of course not. Is that sort of evidence foolproof? Of course not (neither is science). They are subject to cognitive bias, misperception, and other distortions. We will talk more about that later. But they are forms of evidence nonetheless.

Some people write off this type of evidence as "mere anecdote." I don't do that. I believe in the old saying, "The plural of anecdote is data." When you have hundreds or thousands of accounts all telling you essentially the same thing, you had better pay attention. That is evidence that *something* is going on.

Many institutions and disciplines rely on this sort of evidence to make crucial decisions. The legal system makes major, life-changing decisions every day based on observational reports and eyewitness accounts. History, journalism, psychology, sociology, and anthropology would hardly exist without these types of evidence. Observational reports, anecdotal cases, and eyewitness reports are foundational to our knowledge and decision-making as a culture.

They are also foundational to your functioning as a human being. Just think for a second about what it would be like, if the only evidence you used to navigate life was controlled scientific experiments published in peer-reviewed studies. You could hardly get out of bed in the morning and make breakfast. Where is the controlled study telling me what to do!

None of this is to derogate the power of carefully controlled scientific experiments. And to be sure, if controlled scientific experiments on this topic existed, I would be presenting them to you. However, with one exception (see the chapter on mediumship), they do not exist.

There are plenty of reasons why that is so. There is a complete lack of funding for such research. Few researchers want to tackle human afterlife research, much less animal afterlife. Any researcher brave or foolhardy enough to wade into questions touching on a potential afterlife will face peer rejection, ridicule, and potential career suicide. (You think science is an objective enterprise that doesn't repress investigation along certain lines? Think again.) There are major experimental design problems – for example, how would you know or measure what animals are experiencing? And finally, serious ethical problems arise whenever you start talking about randomizing or controlling variables related to death.

For all those reasons and more, there are no controlled, scientific experiments on animal afterlife (with the one exception just mentioned). If you are waiting for that, don't hold your breath. You'll be visiting the afterlife yourself long before it happens (so I guess you will find out before the researchers do).

I am going with the evidence available, which comes in the form of personal experience, observational data, and eye-witness accounts. I am not pretending that those forms of evidence are equivalent to controlled scientific experiments, published in peer-reviewed journals. Of course not. I am just saying that they constitute evidence. They should not be brushed off as "mere anecdote" – especially when hundreds or thousands of people are reporting similar experiences.

Who is This Book For (and Not)?

I intend the book for these sorts of people:

- o Those who love animals and wonder whether they survive death in some form.

- o Those who believe in animal afterlife but would like to see some evidence and argument in support of that belief.

- o People who believe in an afterlife for humans but not for animals (as long as they are open to contrary views).

- o People who are just curious about the subject.

On the other hand, this book is probably *not* for these sorts of people:

- o Hardcore skeptic/materialists who believe that all the afterlife literature is bunk – fraud, hallucinations of a dying brain™, grief-fueled reunion fantasies, misperception, etc.

- o People who only consider controlled scientific experiments to be evidence, and nothing else really counts.

- o Very conservative, fundamentalist Christians, who may be uncomfortable with some of the arguments and evidence.

Regarding the last item: Christians come in all shapes and sizes, and I am sure that many will be open to what I am saying. But some conservative, fundamentalist Christians been taught that only humans have souls, or that mediums are dangerous. They will probably be uncomfortable with much of what I say. If you have that sort of religious orientation, I would suggest you check out books that approach this topic from a Bible-based perspective.

There are many. I found Gary Kurz's *Cold Noses at the Pearly Gates* to be a decent read, many years ago.

Who Am I, and Why Should You Trust Me?

Well, I'm Ed Anderson, a gentleman and a scholar (not really). I don't expect you to trust me, because you don't know me.

I'll tell you a little about myself, though, so you have some sense of where I'm coming from. I'm 61. I retired a few years ago, after a career as a clinical psychologist.

Dogs

I love animals. I'm more of a dog person than a cat person. I like cats, but they make me sneeze. I have a good relationship with squirrels, although I suspect they only love me for my peanuts. I like most animals.

I've lost two dogs to whom I was very close: Boomer and Anna. Boomer died about 15 years ago. It broke my heart. I was stunned at how deep and profound my love could be for a dog. Anna died 4 years ago. I loved Anna deeply, and my grief was intense – but it was also shorter, and more elevated somehow, more spiritual.

I attribute the difference to my greater belief in animal afterlife at the time of Anna's death. I had read more of the literature by then, and I was convinced of animal afterlife. That conviction changed my grief experience. That is part of why I wanted to write the book. I wanted to let other people know about the literature that helped me to believe in animal afterlife. I hoped their grief could be softened and elevated, in the same way mine was.

I had some strange experiences after both of my dogs died. I won't go into detail here, because I don't want my own experience to be the focus, but I will mention that I experienced unexplained movement in the bedsheets, depression on a pillow where my dog used to lie, and a physically tangible sense of my dog's body pressing into mine while sitting in an chair. I also experienced visual anomalies and odd coincidences.

Spirituality

You may be wondering where I'm coming from, spiritually. I wonder that myself sometimes. I won't go into detail, because it's a long story, but briefly, I was raised Catholic, lost my faith at 13, and spent the next 20 years atheist/agnostic. At age 35, I came to believe in God and the afterlife.

There were several steps in that process, which I won't go into. I will mention, though, that I was a hard sell. I'm an analytical guy, skeptical by nature, even cynical at times. I had spent my entire adolescence and early adulthood as an atheist/agnostic. I had a long-time interest in science; I had doctoral-level education on scientific methods and experimental design; I had published some research. Because of my psychology training, I also had lots of education in how people fool themselves.

So, I was way past the point of being persuaded by simple appeals to feeling, faith, or scripture. I needed to be convinced by reason and evidence. I don't mean that feeling didn't play a role. It certainly did. In particular, I remember my sense of shame and regret over having been wrong for so long. On the other hand, there was a tremendous lightening.

I spent the next decade or so wandering. In some ways, I suppose I am still wandering. "All who wander are not lost," as they say, although I admit sometimes I still feel a bit lost. I have tried to wedge myself into various forms of Christianity, and at times, I have managed to do that. Ultimately, though, I don't think organized religion and me are a good fit.

I don't like to put myself in a box, but I probably belong in the one marked "spiritual but not religious," although I disavow the woo-woo connotations. I am basically a seeker, still exploring. I certainly don't have all the answers.

When it comes to spiritual questions, I am biased. I admit that. I believe in a God of some sort, although I find him/her/it very hard to define and understand. I believe in an afterlife of some sort, although not the traditional heaven/hell version. I find some of the afterlife literature credible – not all of it, of course, but some. I wouldn't have written the book otherwise. And I believe that animals have an afterlife. My beliefs are based primarily on evidence, reason, and personal experience.

My bias will seep into how I present the material. That is unavoidable. The best I can do is to acknowledge my bias and try to reign it in. But I have a point of view, and I'm here to express it. No apologies for that.

I will give some attention to skeptical objections, but I will not try to thoroughly represent their side of the argument. I am not interested in doing that, and if I tried, this would be a very different book – a very long book, and one I would not want to write. Others have dealt with most of the skeptical objections already. I don't want to tread that old ground again. And besides, the hardcore skeptical/materialist crowd already dominates the media. They don't need my help in getting their voices heard.

Although I do have my biases, I am not trying to "sell" you on anything. Believe what you like. I am not a pitchman for animal afterlife. I am just here to present some evidence and arguments, in the hope that it might help some people and animals. If you don't find what I say persuasive, that is okay with me.

.

Chapter 2

Overview of the Evidence

I want to give you an overview of the areas of evidence I have included and excluded. I would also like to make two suggestions for how to read the material that follows.

Areas Included and Excluded

I included evidence from the following areas of the afterlife literature:

- o Near-death experiences (NDEs)
- o Visual after-death communications (ADCs)
- o Auditory, tactile, and olfactory ADCs
- o Mediumship
- o Physical mediumship
- o Deathbed visions (DBVs)
- o Ghost reports
- o Out-of-body experiences (OBEs)
- o Electronic voice phenomena (EVP)
- o Spirit photography

On the other hand, I excluded the following types of evidence:

- o "Signs" or strange coincidences
- o Strange animal behavior
- o Evidence of psychic abilities in animals
- o Dreams

Some people might wonder why I chose to exclude those areas, so I will explain briefly.

Signs

Many people report "signs" or strange coincidences after the death of a pet. Although these experiences can be subjectively powerful, they are usually not persuasive to the outside observer. That is part of why I excluded them. I also found many of them to have a "reaching" quality.

I do not mean to disparage those experiences. They may speak in a personal vocabulary that only the experiencer can appreciate. I have had these experiences myself, and some of them have knocked me over. There are tens of thousands of such reports, so I am sure *something* strange is going on. But I decided to leave them out, because their subjective quality tends to leave other people unimpressed – at least in my experience.

Strange Animal Behavior

Some people reported strange animal reactions, which they interpreted to be evidence of an animal spirit nearby. For example, a man might report that his beagle was barking at a spot in the living room where a recently deceased dog used to lie. He sees and hears nothing that might account for the dog barking. He infers that the beagle is perceiving the spirit of the other dog; and that is what he is barking at.

I was intrigued by those accounts, but I excluded them because they rely on human inferences about animal experience. We just aren't very good at knowing what animals are experiencing, especially when they are acting strangely. It would be different if the beagle could give us a verbal report of his experience, but that isn't going to happen.

I included reports where the animal reaction served as secondary support for a human experience. For instance, if the man was having an ADC about the deceased dog, and the beagle started acting strangely at the same time, then I included that. I excluded reports that relied completely on inferences about an animal's behavior.

Psychic Abilities in Animals

Some literature, including some scientific research, supports the theory that animals may have psychic abilities. For example, the biologist Rupert Sheldrake has done a series of controlled experiments showing that some dogs are able to know in advance when their owners are coming home, even when the times of arrival are randomized and there are no external cues.[1] Sheldrake has also talked about other potential animal psychic abilities in his work. In addition, Emma Heathcote-Jones has compiled many accounts suggesting psychic abilities in animals.[2]

I do not find this hard to believe. Given that we have good research suggesting that some humans exhibit psychic abilities (e.g., remote viewing, telepathy), why couldn't animals? After all, they often have much better-developed senses than we do; why not a much-better developed sixth sense as well?

I decided to exclude that line of evidence, though, because it doesn't bear directly on questions of animal afterlife. Now, you could argue that psychic abilities makes an afterlife more likely or plausible, since psychic phenomena suggest that consciousness is non-local (i.e., not confined to the brain). But that is a rather indirect argument. I wanted to focus on more direct evidence.

Dreams

Many people have reported dreams in which they encounter deceased loved ones, including animals. These dreams feel different to them than normal dreams. For instance, they may feel more intense and real than a normal dream. They may involve a simple, ordinary encounter, without any of the weirdness or plot twists that accompany a normal dream. They are more memorable than an ordinary dream.

These are interesting events. I have had several of these dreams myself, and they do feel distinctly different from normal dreams, in the ways just described. However, I decided to exclude them, because, although they may be subjectively compelling, they are too easy to write off as "just a dream."

———————

Before getting to the evidence, I would like to make two suggestions for how to read what follows.

Parallels to the General Literature

In each of the areas (NDE, ADC, etc.), the animal afterlife literature is just one small niche in a much larger literature, which is almost entirely focused on human beings. In some of these areas, the literature goes back decades if not centuries. Faced with skeptical scrutiny, careful researchers have meticulously ruled out many alternative explanations. This is more true of some areas (e.g., NDE and mediumship) than in others, but all of them have received careful attention by dedicated researchers.

Once you appreciate that the breadth of the general literature and see how it has addressed many skeptical counterclaims, you will see the animal afterlife literature in a different context. You will see it as part of a greater whole.

17

In that way, you will be able to take your confidence in what the general literature shows and apply some of that to the animal literature. These are just two aspects of the same phenomena, after all, not two unrelated phenomena. For instance, when "deceased" animals show up in NDEs, ADCs, or mediumship readings, they do so in the same way that "deceased" humans do.

I understand that most readers will not be acquainted with the larger literature, so they will not appreciate the point I am trying to make here. That's okay. If you are interested in exploring the general literature in any of these areas, I have provided resources in the footnotes for each chapter. I believe that most people who take the time to read the general literature in depth will find it persuasive. If you understand the general literature, you can place what follows in a broader context.

This may also help in areas where the published evidence for animal afterlife is rather thin. For example, the section on EVPs contains only a dozen accounts involving animals. You may think, "Twelve accounts? Is that it? Big deal." But there is a larger body of work on EVPs, and it provides some evidence that human consciousness survives bodily death. If you appreciate that, then you will be able to fit the animal stories into that context. There is no reason to suppose that the general literature applies only to human beings and not animals. Of course, some areas have better quality investigations than others, and some provide better evidence of the afterlife than others.

I wish I could summarize the general afterlife literature for you, so you could better appreciate what I am saying, but that would take me 24 volumes and several lifetimes, and I ain't getting any younger. The best I can do is to point you to some resources, so that you can start exploring the subject on your own, if you like.

The White Crow

I'd also like to suggest that you consider the "white crow" principle. The idea here is that we don't need all the evidence to be valid; we just need one part of it to be.

Imagine that you see a bunch of crows, and they are all black. After a good while of seeing black crow after black crow, it would be reasonable to suppose that all crows are black. This is called inductive reasoning, and we use it all the time. It is the basis for most generalizations.

There is a problem with it, though. William James, the famous philosopher and psychologist, put it this way:

> *If you wish to upset the law that all crows are black, you mustn't seek to show that no crows are; it is enough to prove one single crow to be white.*

If someone believes all crows are black, then all you need to do, to disprove that belief, is show them a single white crow. Actually, it could be green, purple, or yellow, but let's stick with white.

When William James said this, he wasn't talking about crows; he was talking about mediums. James and a long list of eminent scientists investigated mediums back in the late 1800s. We tend to think of people in the 19th century as naïve compared to us, but these were careful scientific researchers, including Nobel prize winners; they had skeptics and aggressive debunkers in their ranks, too.

This was during the heyday of mediumship. Frauds abounded – unscrupulous people were trying to cash in on the craze. Harry Houdini and others exposed many of these frauds. So did James and other investigators. These were the "black crows."

After seeing mediumistic fraud after fraud exposed, it would be reasonable to conclude, "All mediums are frauds." Many people today do the same: all the crows are black.

As James pointed out, though, no number of fraudulent mediums says anything about the possibility of a genuine medium. James found his white crow in Leonora Piper, but that is another story.[3]

I want to suggest that you consider the "white crow" principle as you read the evidence. This principle doesn't apply just to mediumship. It applies to all of the areas, both individually and collectively.

Here is how it works. Begin with the hardcore skeptical, materialist position: animals do not have an afterlife; all the so-called evidence for animal afterlife is explicable as fraud, misperception, hallucination or the like. All crows are black. In order to disprove that:

- o Every NDE account does not have to be valid ("valid" in the sense of providing real evidence of animal afterlife); it is enough that one is.

- o Every mediumistic report does not need to be valid; it is enough that one is.

- o Every After-Death Communication (ADC) report does not need to be valid; just one does.

And so on. The same principle applies to all of the areas of evidence. We don't need all the reports to be valid; we just need one of them to be. That is enough to disprove the proposition that "animals do not have an afterlife; all of the so-called evidence is just fraud, misperception, hallucination, or the like." Since there are only two options – either animals have an afterlife or they don't – then disproving the one validates the other. If we have one white crow, that is enough to demonstrate animal afterlife – at least in that one case.

A single valid case, then, is enough to demonstrate that animals (at least one of them, anyhow) have an afterlife. This is not lowering the bar; this is logic. If you have a single valid counterexample, then all crows cannot be black.

I mention the white crow principle because many of us, myself included, are skeptical by nature. As you read, you will probably find yourself doubting the validity of certain cases. That is fine. I don't buy all of them myself. The point is, they don't all have to be valid. In order to demonstrate that animals have an afterlife, you don't need every report to be valid; you just need one of them to be. You just need one white crow. Personally, I think we've got a flock of white crows flying around in these pages, but you will decide for yourself.

—————————

I encourage you to keep those two things in mind as you read what follows – this is just one small part of a larger whole, and keep an eye out for white crows.

Chapter 3

Near-Death Experiences

There are over 200 peer-reviewed studies published on near-death experiences (NDEs) in scientific journals. Many researchers have spent decades studying NDEs – Dr. Jeffrey Long, Dr. Janice Holden, Dr. Pim von Lommel, Dr. Bruce Greyson, Dr. Kenneth Ring, and Dr. Raymond Moody, to name a few. Many of them began as curious skeptics, unable to ignore what their patients reported. Most ended as cautious believers, concluding that, based on the evidence available, the best explanation is that consciousness survives clinical death of the body.

There are also tens of thousands of reports of NDE experiences from people of all walks of life – scientists, mailmen, physicians, clerks, lawyers, nurses, whatever. They come from people who are devoutly religious, and they come from atheists and agnostics. They come from all corners of the globe, from people of all faiths or no faith. The remarkable thing is how similar their experiences are. Further, many of the reports include accurate observations while "dead" that the person could not have known about (e.g., details of the medical procedure, conversations elsewhere in the hospital).

I cannot summarize that literature, because it is massive, but I encourage you to explore it.[1] Most people who take the time to seriously, sincerely explore the subject come away convinced that something very strange is going on – something that cannot be explained by medical science, psychology, neuroscience, or the laws of nature as we currently understand them. Attempts to explain them away as hallucinations, drug effects, wishful thinking, etc., do not hold up.

Animals in NDEs

All the major researchers on NDEs confirm that animals appear regularly in NDE accounts. People who undergo clinical death and experience an NDE will sometimes see their departed pets on the "other side."

Dr. Raymond Moody, the grandfather of NDE research, confirms it. So does Dr. Kenneth Ring, a second-generation pioneer in NDE research. And so do Dr. Jeffrey Long and Penny Sartori, to name a couple modern researchers. No NDE researcher I know has failed to report that animals – usually pets – appear in NDEs.

Do you find NDE reports credible as evidence for an afterlife? If so, then NDEs provide good support for animals existing in that afterlife, because the experts in the field consistently report that animals appear in NDEs.

How Many?

I found 62 specific cases described in the literature.[3] Although the experts confirm that animals appear in NDEs, the number of cases described in the literature is not as large as one might hope.

Woops, Forgot to Ask

Scott Smith, a journalist who explored the question of animal afterlife[2], noticed this. He asked a researcher why animals were not mentioned as often as you might expect. The researcher replied that they simply had not inquired about animals as a part of the interviews. Smith stated, "It turned out that the lack of reports about animals in the hereafter was due to the fact that researchers had not bothered to ask anyone about this issue." Anyone who has done interview or questionnaire-based research knows that if you don't ask a question about something, you are not likely to hear about it.

That is a pattern in afterlife literature generally. As I mentioned earlier, animals tend to be an afterthought. I don't fault the researchers for this. Naturally, they are interested in the big questions first – can consciousness operate independently of the brain? Is there evidence of an afterlife at all? They aren't thinking about the specific issue of animal survival.

They are focused on the general issue, and they are looking at it from a human perspective. All the researchers are human; all the experiencers giving verbal reports are human; all the people writing books and giving speeches are human. If dogs were doing the research, we would probably wonder why human beings aren't better represented.

Despite all that, animals still manage to show up in NDEs – poking their heads through the afterlife curtain, so to speak.

Published Accounts vs. the Internet

As I said, I found 62 specific, published descriptions of animals appearing in NDEs. However, I want to clarify that this number (62) only represents the specific, published accounts.

For the most part, I restricted my search to books, avoiding stories posted on the internet. Perhaps this was self-handicapping, because I thereby radically restricted the number of reports available. In today's world, so much gets expressed on the internet; books are old-fashioned tech.

There are thousands of NDEs posted on the internet. There are tens of thousands of afterlife accounts of all sorts published on the internet. However, I did not have the stamina to deal with all that. I restricted myself mostly to books, just to keep my job manageable. I'm retired after all. I don't want to stress myself. If I went down the internet rabbit hole, looking for every afterlife report I could find, scouring hundreds of Facebook groups and websites, I would never finish. Gathering it all up would be an endless task.

And maybe this is just my prejudice, but I suspect that reports in books have a slightly higher credibility than stories posted on the internet. I am not saying that people who post stories on the internet are making them up, but anyone can post anything on the internet, often anonymously. In a book, at least you have the author serving as some kind of credibility check; and sometimes, the person's name and location are published as well, which reduces incentives for lying.

Although I excluded most internet sources, I did want to include Nderf.org, at least. Nderf.org isn't just a Facebook group; it's the largest collection of NDEs in the world. The website is run by Jeffrey Long, MD, who is a prominent NDE researcher, and his wife, Jody Long. Nderf.org currently has over 5000 NDE reports posted.

The people reporting NDEs at nderf.org are required to fill out a long, extensive questionnaire. That tends to weed out people who just want to troll the process. People who take the time and energy to fill out these questionnaires get nothing for it – no attention, no "likes," no responses. Their story just gets filed in the heap with all the others. So there is little incentive for just making something up. Jeff Long also does basic screening for frauds and trolls. He stated that only 2% of the reports fall in those categories, and they are removed from the database.

Unfortunately, the nderf.org database is not searchable by specific terms (e.g., "animals"). Although they have over 5000 NDEs, I could not figure out how many contained animals. It seemed to me that I would need to read through 5000 long, detailed narratives, to figure that out. I didn't have that kind of time.

Fortunately, Jimmy Akin came to the rescue. Jimmy is senior apologist at Catholic Answers and host of *Jimmy Akin's Mysterious World*, a podcast that explores paranormal topics. Jimmy used his google-fu to search the nderf.org database.

Here is what Jimmy said:

> *It turns out that nderf.org is archived in such a way that Google searches its individual NDE accounts, and so it's possible to put in words like dog and site:nderf.org and get results. I therefore tried this with words like "dog," "cat," "horse," and "pet" and got lots of results.*
>
> *There were 594 NDE pages referring to dogs, 194 referring to cats, 128 referring to horses, and 144 mentioning pets.*

I am grateful to Jimmy for his help. Let's break those numbers down. Although the total number is 1060, that overestimates the number of unique cases, because there will be overlap in the categories. To get the number of unique cases, we need to subtract the "pets" category (144), since that is likely a redundant term. For instance, people often use the terms "pet" and "dog" when referring to the same animal. We may lose a few unique cases that way, but I prefer to be conservative in my counts.

We also need to avoid double-counting cases in which someone mentions more than one animal in a single report. For instance, a woman may report seeing both her dog and cat in an NDE. Even though two different animals are mentioned, that is one NDE report, not two. We don't want to double-count a single report.

How many cases like this are there, where someone is reporting both a dog and a cat in a single NDE, and thus getting counted twice? We cannot know for sure, but we can make an educated guess.

We know that 594 people reported seeing dogs. We know that the total number of unique cases cannot be less than that. We can start there. We also know that 194 people reported seeing cats. How many of them also saw a dog? Well, although some people own both a cat and a dog, most people are "dog people" or "cat people," preferring one or the other. If we assume that two-thirds of the people who saw cats are "cat people" who did not also own a dog, then 130 people (two-thirds of 194) saw a cat but not a dog. If we add those two figures together, we get 724 unique cases. There may be cases where someone saw both a dog and a cat, but we have counted it only once, not twice.

What about the 128 horses? How many of the people seeing horses did not also report seeing either a cat or a dog? That is hard to say. I suspect that most horse owners also own a dog or a cat, so they could report seeing both or all three. Let's assume that only a third of the reports are of only a horse. That would be 42 additional cases, bringing the total to 766.

I would estimate, then, that of the approximately 5000 NDE reports in the nderf.org database, 766 of them contain animals. That is 15% of the total.

Unpublished Reports

There are also hundreds of unpublished reports of animals in NDEs, sitting in researchers' file drawers. Scott Smith spoke with Cambridge psychiatrist Dr. Milton Hadley. Dr. Hadley has spent many years researching NDEs. Dr. Hadley told Smith that he had "hundreds of accounts of pet encounters during NDEs," but these were all unpublished.[2]

Why unpublished? Because they are embedded within long narratives based on interviews and questionnaires. Publishing the accounts would be impractical – they would be a nightmare to edit into readable form, and few people would want to read a huge volume of case reports.

How many other NDE researchers have hundreds of unpublished cases in their file drawers (or on their computers)? I doubt Dr. Hadley is the only one. I suspect he is the rule, not the exception. NDE research is often based on interviews and questionnaires, and what sees publication are summaries of those findings, not the raw data itself. No one is publishing the raw case reports; they remain in storage. Considering that dozens of researchers have been working in this area for decades, there must be thousands of unpublished cases.

How many of the thousands of unpublished cases contain reports of animals? We cannot know for sure, but we could estimate, based on the nderf.org percentage (15%), that there are hundreds.

————————

Counts

- I found 62 specific animal NDE encounters in the literature.

- Of the 5000+ NDE reports in the nderf.org database, an estimated 766 feature animals. That is 15% of the total.

- There are likely thousands of unpublished NDE cases stored in researchers' files. If we use the 15% figure above, that would mean there are hundreds of unpublished NDE cases featuring animals.

If we wanted to, we could also extrapolate that 15% to the total number of NDEs reported worldwide, but that is enough. You get the point: animals appear regularly and often in NDEs.

I'll share some examples.

Happy Returns

Here is an example of a very simple NDE appearance of an animal.

> I saw my deceased dog from my childhood bounding towards me. I remember exclaiming her name at the top of my lungs as I saw her bounding towards me. It was overwhelmingly wonderful. I felt completely at peace and totally happy. I was so excited to see her again, and I did not question the experience at the time. It was as if she had never died and she had always been waiting for me to wake up from my nap in the grass.[4]

If you are familiar with the NDE literature, you will recognize this pattern: a happy reunion with a deceased loved one. This is standard NDE stuff. No two NDEs are identical, but they do follow a common pattern, and a happy reunion is one of their common features. Usually, this reunion occurs in a peaceful setting, often one of natural beauty. The "deceased" loved one appears healthy and usually younger than when last seen on Earth.

Typically, the happy reunion is with a human being, but here the loved one is a dog. It follows the same pattern. He wakes up in a peaceful meadow. He has feelings of happiness, love, and excitement about the reunion. The dog is in good health.

Whatever is happening with "deceased" human beings appearing in NDEs is also happening with "deceased" animals. The dynamic is the same. These are not two unrelated phenomena – human beings and animals – they are just two aspects of the same process. To the degree that you find the general NDE literature credible, you can transfer some of that credibility to the animal accounts. That is, if you believe that the general NDE literature provides support for belief in an afterlife, that can give you more confidence in the animal NDE accounts. (This is one advantage of becoming familiar with the general NDE literature, which I encourage you to do.)

"If you think you'll never see them [your pets] again, you're mistaken." - veteran NDEr Dannion Brinkley

NDEs with Additional Validity Features

Beyond those simple, standard accounts of happy reunions, we also have cases that provide additional features that enhance believability or credibility. These accounts provide evidence that something beyond just imagination or hallucination is going on. There are hundreds of such cases in the general NDE literature. Here, I will confine myself to the animal cases.

They come in two main forms:

1. The person reports seeing an animal "on the other side," but does not know that the animal has died. If the person does not know the animal is "dead," why would he or she hallucinate it being on the other side?

2. The person sees an animal with whom he or she has no emotional connection. These cases help rule out the theory that NDEs are just comforting hallucinations, designed to alleviate separation and grief.

Didn't Know They Were Dead (DKD)

During some NDEs, a person sees someone on "the other side" that they did not know was dead. For example, a man might see an uncle in an NDE, and upon being revived, he is confused, because he believes that uncle to be alive. Later, he learns that his uncle had died suddenly a few days prior to his NDE. He did not know about this. It is difficult to explain why he would see him on "the other side," if he did not realize the uncle had passed.

I call these "DKD" cases, short for "didn't know they were dead." There are many DKD reports in the general NDE literature, featuring human beings.

We have some in the animal literature as well. I will give you two examples, both drawn from Scott Smith's book, *The Soul of Your Pet*. Smith is a journalist who investigated the issue of animal survival.

The first case involves a woman who was in a coma for several days, then declared dead. Apparently, reports of her death were greatly exaggerated, because five hours later, she sat bolt upright in the bed, shouting.

She reported having an NDE. During the NDE, she saw her mother greet her cat. This was puzzling, because although she knew that her mother was dead, she thought her cat was still alive. The cat had been alive when she entered the coma.[5]

Why is she seeing her cat, whom she believed to be alive, on the other side? Furthermore, why is she seeing her deceased mother greeting the cat, as if the cat had just arrived, when the cat had just recently died?

If an NDE is just a comforting hallucination, why would you imagine your living cat in the hereafter? That would not be comforting; that would be confusing. Indeed, it was confusing to her, until someone informed her that her cat had passed away while she was in the coma.

Perhaps, during her coma, she overheard someone at bedside remark on the cat's death. Some people in coma can sometimes hear things said at bedside, so that is a possibility we should consider. But if that was the case, why was the woman puzzled by the cat's appearance with her mother? Wouldn't she have found the appearance understandable, if she knew the cat had passed? Wouldn't she have found it comforting, to see mom welcoming her cat into the afterlife? Why did she need someone else to tell her that cat had passed away, if she already knew that?

You will make up your own mind about these cases, of course, but I find it more plausible to believe that she saw the cat "on the other side" because, contrary to her expectations, that is where the cat was.

––––––––––

Here is another example. A man was pronounced clinically dead. He had an NDE. In the NDE, he saw another man, unknown to him. The man was holding a cat, also unknown to him. He found this strange and puzzling. He did not recognize either the man or the cat.

Sometime later, the man was looking through some old family photos belonging to his parents. Among the piles of photos, he happened across a picture of a man holding a cat. He was startled: it was the man and cat from his NDE.

He still had no idea who the man or the cat were. He had never seen them before. He questioned his parents about it, and eventually, they confessed that the man in the photo was his biological brother. The man was adopted. Although his parents had told him long ago about his adoptive status, they had never told him that he had a biological brother. They had hidden that information from him his entire life.

And the cat? It belonged to his brother. At the time of his NDE, both his brother and the cat were long since deceased.[5]

So, this man died, had an NDE, and saw a man and a cat that he did not know existed, much less died. He did not know he had a brother. He did not know his brother had a cat. And he did not know either of them were dead. And yet, he saw both "on the other side" in his NDE.

He insisted that he had never seen either of them before. His parents had carefully hidden this information from him. It was only much later, combing through old photos stashed in his parents' closet, then questioning his parents about the matter, that he discovered their identities.

How can one explain this? Why would this man hallucinate a person he had never known, much less a cat he had never known, during an NDE? Their appearance was not comforting; it was confusing. Furthermore, hallucinations by definition are unreal, and yet this man obtained information that was later verified to be true – something he had no knowledge of at the time.

The main star of the NDE is the man's biological brother, but let's not forget about the cat. Why would he "hallucinate" a cat in the hereafter that he did not know had died – heck, never even knew existed?

Those are two DKD examples. There are other stories like it in the animal literature, in which pets not known to be deceased appear on "the other side," then later verified to have recently passed. The human NDE literature contains many such accounts as well, which cannot be dismissed as mere hallucinations.

No Emotional Attachment

During the happy reunion phase of an NDE, most people will see loved ones with whom they have a strong emotional connection. Sometimes these are spiritual beings of some sort. Skeptics sometimes dismiss these happy reunions as nothing more than comforting fantasies, designed to alleviate separation and grief over the loss of those loved ones.

I have never quite understood that explanation myself. Why would someone on the brink of death need to be relieved of grief over the loss of loved ones? In most cases, these loved ones have passed away years or even decades ago. At the moment of death, why would you be troubled over the death of your grandmother, years ago? Do you not have other things to worry about?

In any case, I want to turn our attention to NDE cases where people see people (or animals) to whom they have no particular emotional attachment. If the happy reunion is nothing more than a hallucination designed to alleviation separation and grief over the loss of a loved one, why would you need such a hallucination in these cases? There is no emotional attachment. There is no grief or felt separation. The "comforting hallucination" explanation doesn't wash.

I'll give you a few brief examples of cases in the NDE literature, where people see animals to whom they have no emotional connection.

One woman reported seeing several different animals in her NDE – cats and dogs, mostly – that she did not know. She said the animals were just "hanging around." She had no emotional attachment to any of them. She was told they were waiting for their human companions to arrive.[5]

Another woman reported an NDE in which she saw a sheep and a goat, neither of which she had known in her normal life.[6]

A third woman reported seeing a deer, a squirrel, and a rabbit in her NDE – none of which she had ever known. [6]

In all these cases, the women had no emotional connection to any of the animals they saw. The animals were just there.

There are more cases like this, but that is a sample. You can't explain those away as being hallucinations designed to alleviate grief or separation. They do no such thing, because there isn't any emotional connection there. The animals are unknown to the people seeing them. There is no grief. These are not deceased loved ones; they are strangers. The people report them in a matter-of-fact way, as neutral observations. The animals are just *there*.

Shared NDEs

NDEs are usually an individual thing. In some cases, though, aspects of the experience are shared. The person at bedside also experiences elements of the NDE. Loved ones or medical personnel at bedside may, for example, see the white light, a tunnel, have a glimpse into what looks like a beautiful heavenly world, may see the dead person step across a boundary, or possibly see other deceased individuals – all standard parts of an NDE experience. This is happening while the dying person is also having an NDE.

These occurrences are called "shared NDEs." They are very difficult to explain away in materialistic terms.[7] Hardcore skeptics routinely default to "hallucinations of a dying brain" as a supposed explanation. Although there is no evidence to support this hypothesis, and significant reason to reject it, it remains the preferred go-to for materialist skeptics; it is pretty much an article of faith.

Shared NDEs are one piece of evidence that counters the "hallucination of a dying brain" hypothesis. If an NDE is the hallucination of a dying brain, why are people at bedside having elements of the same NDE experience, while the dying person is also having an NDE? Those people are not dying. Presumably, they are not even ill. They are just family members or medical personnel who happen to be there at the time of the person's (temporary) passing. They are also having an NDE-like experience, coinciding with the one the person "dying" is having. How can their experience be the "product of a dying brain"?

Stories involving shared NDEs with animals are difficult to locate. This is for a very simple reason. Animals cannot verbally report their experience, so we cannot know when they are having an NDE. So we cannot correlate the animal's experience with any NDE-like experience for people at bedside.

I did find one suggestive case, though, documented by Niki Shanahan. After a protracted illness, a woman's cat, Samantha, was dying. The woman reported:

> *Finally, she gave an almost joyous loud cry and sank to her feet, breathing her last. Almost immediately, I heard a loud rushing sound and saw a huge white light, which became almost like a large movie screen. There was a scene of a small stream, across from which was a brilliant landscape of green foliage and gorgeous flower.*
>
> *Suddenly, our Samantha was seen carefully stepping on stones, crossing the stream. She reached the other side, turned and looked back at me, and then bounded up the hill on the other side, like a kitten, looking back once more before continuing on.*
>
> *There was a sudden popping sound, and the vision disappeared, and I was left with Samantha's lifeless form beside me, but with a new and relaxed appearance on her face.* [8]

The woman reports many features common to NDEs: the white light, the beautiful nature scene, the transitional image (crossing the stream), and the youthful appearance ("looking like a kitten"). Did she share in her cat's transition somehow? We cannot know, because we don't have the cat's side of the story. But it does resemble what is reported in shared NDEs.

Post-NDE Personality Changes

To me, one of the most interesting features of NDEs is how they change the person who experiences them. Hallucinations don't generally do that, and if they do, they usually do it for the worse. An NDE, though, is often followed by dramatic changes in core values, personality, and lifestyle. These personality and value changes align with what happens in other spiritually transformative experiences – for example, the person becomes less materialistic, less concerned with status, and more concerned with helping others.

This is one reason to believe NDEs represent more than just comforting hallucinations. Hallucinations rarely result in permanent, positive changes in people's values and lifestyle. Yet it happens routinely with NDEs.[9]

We do not have many well-documented cases of this happening with animals – in part for the reason I mentioned above: we do not know when animals have an NDE, because they cannot verbally report their experiences.

However, Kim Sheridan, who wrote a wonderful book on evidence for animal afterlife, shared this:

> *I have encountered a number of cases of animals who have had dramatic personality changes after undergoing major surgery or having other experiences resulting in close brushes with death. Much like humans who have undergone these experiences and returned with a more peaceful, loving outlook on life, these animals likewise seem to radiate a profound peace and are much more loving than they were before, even those who have previously had behavioral problems. I can't help but wonder if these animals have returned from NDEs as well.[10]*

Was the personality of those animals changed by their medical condition, or by an NDE? It is hard to say, but it is an idea worth considering. If human beings are profoundly changed by an NDE, why couldn't an animal be as well?

———————

NDE Wrap Up

To recap the main points:

- All major NDE researchers report that animals repeatedly show up in NDEs.

- I found 62 published, specific reports of animals appearing in NDEs.

- With Jimmy Akin's help, I estimated that there are about 766 NDE reports featuring animals in the nderf.org database (15%).

- There are likely hundreds of other cases of animals appearing in NDEs, stored in researchers' files, unpublished.
- Being familiar with the general NDE literature will give you greater confidence in the validity of animal reports. I encourage you to acquaint yourself with that literature.

- There are DKD cases, in which people see animals "on the other side" that they did not realize had died – in some cases, they didn't even know they existed. Standard skeptical explanations cannot account for these cases.

o There are cases in which an NDEr sees animals to whom they have no emotional connection. These are also difficult to explain away in standard skeptical terms.

o Although such cases are limited by animals' inability to give verbal reports, we have some suggestions of shared NDE and personality transformations with animals, similar to what we see in the human NDE literature.

In my estimation, the NDE literature, taken as a whole, provides substantial support for belief in animal afterlife.

Chapter 4

Visual ADCs

After the death of a loved one, many people report experiences in which they see, feel, hear, or otherwise sense the presence of that departed loved one. In the afterlife literature, these experiences are termed After-Death Communications (ADCs). Skeptics dismiss them as grief-induced hallucinations.

Reports of such experiences date back at least 2000 years. We see them in much of the ancient literature. Thousands of people have reported visual ADCs of "dead" people. The reports exist across cultures and throughout recorded history.

Bill and Judy Guggenheim spent 7 years researching ADCs in the United States and Canada. They compiled more than 3300 first-hand accounts and interviewed 2000 people from all walks of life.[1] They classified reports into the following categories:

- Visual (e.g., seeing a departed person)
- Auditory (e.g., hearing a voice)
- Tactile (e.g., feeling their touch)
- Olfactory (e.g., smelling a fragrance associated with them)
- Experiences of "presence"
- Physical or electronic phenomena
- Dream encounters
- "Signs" or strange coincidences

Other people besides the Guggenheims have compiled ADCs and present many additional accounts.[2] The Guggenheims estimated that 20% of the US population has had an ADC of some type.

I review visual ADCs featuring "deceased" animals in this chapter. I will save auditory, tactile, and olfactory ADCs for later. I will leave the other sorts of ADC experiences out (signs, dreams, etc.). I found plenty of them in the animal literature, but for reasons explained in the Introduction, I chose to omit them.

A common visual ADC would be seeing your recently deceased grandmother at the foot of your bed. Most people feel comforted when this happens, although some freak out. ADC experiencers often comment that the visual ADC was accompanied by a feeling of love and a reassurance that the "deceased" person was still alive in spirit. Indeed, that is what many believe the ADC's function to be – it serves as a message from the "deceased" to those left behind that they are okay.

How Many?

In the published literature, I found 112 visual ADCs involving animals – 72 dogs, 33 cats, 4 horses, one bird, one rabbit, and a rat.[3]

The frequency corresponds to the types of animals people keep as pets – dogs being the most popular, followed by cats, then horses, birds, rabbits, and rats. The exception here would be fish.

Fish are one of the more common pets, but we don't see many fish ADCs.

Animals in ADCs are almost always pets. I didn't see any ADCs involving wild animals. Wild animals do occasionally appear in NDE reports and ghost/apparition reports, but I didn't find any in ADCs. That makes sense, because ADCs usually happen in the context of an emotional bond between a person and an animal pet. Recall that many ADC experiencers report that the ADC seemed to convey a message of love and reassurance – a very personal message. There are a couple of exceptions to that rule, which I'll get to shortly, but, in general, ADCs happen in the presence of a strong emotional bond. And there wouldn't usually be an emotional bond with a wild animal.

As I mentioned, I found 112 visual ADCs featuring animals in the literature. I did not read all of the ADC literature, though, so I might have missed a few (that goes for all the areas we surveyed; I read what I could, but I did not read everything).

There are likely hundreds more reports on the internet. For instance, adcrf.org is an internet website that catalogs ADCs. It is run by Dr. Jeff Long and his wife Jody, the same people who run nderf.org. Adcrf.org currently contains 1747 ADCs. How many of those feature animals? Dr. Julia Assante stated on her blog that the Longs informed her that 16% of the ADC reports involve pets.[4] That is similar to the percentage we estimated for NDE reports of animals in the nderf.org database (15%).

If 16% of the adcrf.org accounts feature animals, then that would amount to 280 reports on that database. Granted, not all them would be visual ADCs; some would be auditory, tactile, etc.

That is only one site where ADC reports can be found. If you check the many pet loss discussion forums, you will see ADC reports being posted continually. People also post ADC reports featuring animals on afterlife discussion forums. If you take the 280 reports from adcrf, then add the hundreds more posted on internet forums, I am confident it would total well over a thousand.

I'm not saying you should believe everything posted on the internet. That would be silly. I'm just saying that ADC reports of "deceased" animals are very common.

We could even take the Guggenheims' estimate that 20% of the US population have had an ADC and combine it with the 16% figure reported by Dr. Assante. That would mean 3.2% of the US population – or over 10 million people – have had an animal ADC, just in the US. However, the Guggenheims used a very broad definition of ADCs that included many phenomena I chose to exclude, so that number is probably an overreach.

Moreover, that would just be an estimate of the number of people who have *experienced* an ADC, not the number who have *reported* that experience. Many people – probably most, in fact – have these sorts of experiences without publicly reporting them. There are many reasons for that. They might consider the experiences too personal to make public. They might not be interested in reporting it publicly. They might doubt its validity.

They might not have the opportunity to report it publicly. Or they might fear ridicule.

By the way, that is true for many of the areas we will survey. The number of *experiences* will greatly outnumber the number of *reported* experiences. I am just tallying the *reported* experiences.

I located 112 visual ADCs involving animals in the published literature. If we include ADC reports on the internet, the number rises by the hundreds and probably reaches well over a thousand.

Let's look at some examples.

Simple Encounters

We begin with the simplest and most common type – a person sees a "deceased" animal, and that's about it. There is nothing in the account to lend it additional credibility (e.g., multiple witnesses). I am calling that a "simple" encounter, because of the simplicity of the report itself.

Of the 112 visual ADCs in the published literature, simple encounters represented 37% of the cases. The other 63% had some element that lent it additional credibility. I'll discuss the latter in a moment. For now, let's stick with the simple cases.

I do not think the 37% figure is representative. It is an underestimate. I have no doubt that simple encounters are the most common type. We are dealing with the published literature, after all, and authors are selective about what they include (otherwise, they would be lousy authors). Anyone who sets out to gather ADC reports will be inundated with simple encounters, but a book full of nothing but simple encounters would be dull. The authors will naturally select for cases have something unusual about them – some feature that lends them authenticity or credibility.

But most ADCs are simple encounters. Here is an example. It comes from Kim Sheridan's book, *Animals and the Afterlife*.

A woman had a dog named Princess. Princess grew old, and one day, the woman had to euthanize her. Shortly afterward, the woman reported the following:

> *I woke up in the middle of the night and Princess was at the foot of the bed, looking at me. She looked so beautiful. I sat up and reached, wanting to hug her, and she disappeared. I wasn't dreaming; I was totally awake. ... I know that when she came to me that night, she did so to let me know that she is okay and that they do continue living on.*[5]

The woman awakens, sees her dog at the foot of the bed, and then, after a moment, it fades. Although she was awakened from sleep, she insists that she was fully awake at the time of the ADC, not dreaming. She feels that the appearance was meant to convey the message that her dog is doing just fine.

That is a simple ADC. Apart from what the woman reports, there is nothing unusual in the account to lend it additional credibility. You either take her word for it, or you don't. That is what I am calling a simple encounter.

Most people assess these cases based on prior belief. Believers in animal afterlife will nod their heads and find her account credible. Hardcore skeptics will dismiss them as misperception, dishonesty, or hallucination. There is nothing besides the simple encounter to add credibility to the account (or subtract from it), so you are left to decide for yourself one way or another. Most people decide based on their previous beliefs.

Although I don't want to press the point too hard, I would like to suggest two reasons why you might grant these simple encounters a bit more credence than you might be inclined to.

First, many of these people consented to have their names and locations published. If you report these experiences openly, you are subjecting yourself to the "giggle factor" so prevalent around these topics; you are opening yourself up to ridicule. If someone is willing to expose themselves to potential embarrassment in order to report an experience, that suggests they are at least reporting their experience honestly.

Second, about a third of the simple encounters I found were actually multiple encounters. That is, the person saw their deceased pet not just once, but several times, often over weeks or months. I counted these multiple experiences as a single ADC, to keep my counts conservative, but the repetition over an extended period of time is significant. Although you might dismiss a single

ADC as the result of fatigue, emotionality, or imagination run amok, it becomes harder to do that when there are multiple experiences, all similar, spread over weeks or months.

Grief-Induced Hallucination?

Before we get to the cases that are not so simple – the cases with additional credibility features – I want to discuss the most common explanation offered by hardcore materialist/skeptics for ADCs. It goes like this: the person is experiencing tremendous grief over the loss of the loved one. In order to relieve that emotional pain, the brain subconsciously generates a fantasied reunion with the deceased loved one. Basically, an ADC is a hallucination cooked up by a distressed brain, designed to reduce grief. The person mistakes the hallucination for reality.

This is an easy line for skeptics/materialists to take, since they are supported in doing so by the medical and psychiatric profession. These professions define an ADC experience as hallucinatory, right out of the gate. They don't even consider that it might be authentic.

The National Institute of Health informs us that "auditory or visual hallucinations of the deceased person are often seen during acute grief." Psychiatry does the same, saying that these types of "hallucinations" are common in grief. In fact, ADCs are considered a symptom of a mental disorder. According to the DSM-5, which is the psychiatric bible used to diagnose mental disorders, "auditory or visual hallucinations of the deceased person" are a symptom of Persistent Complex Bereavement Disorder. Maybe you need some psychiatric medication.

"Hallucination" is a psychiatric term. I am retired now, but I spent my career in a psychiatry-adjacent field, clinical psychology, dominated by the medical/psychiatric model. In that model, hallucinations are almost always associated with mental illness, and serious mental illness at that – bipolar disorder, schizophrenia, severe major depression, thought disorders; they can also occur during acute drug intoxication or withdrawal. If you are hallucinating, that is not good. It means something has gone seriously wrong with your brain.

Here is what the Cleveland Clinic has to say:

A hallucination is a false perception of objects or events involving your senses: sight, sound, smell, touch and taste. Hallucinations seem real, but they're not. Chemical reactions and/or abnormalities in your brain cause hallucinations.

Got it? An ADC is a hallucination, and a hallucination is a false perception, caused by "chemical reactions and/or abnormalities in your brain." It's all in your head, you poor thing.

That is simply the automatic assumption in the psychiatric and medical community: ADCs are hallucinatory. Those professions give zero consideration to the possibility that ADCs might reflect something genuine – i.e., a perception of something real, not hallucinatory. That possibility is not even mentioned, much less considered. The ADC is defined right from the start as a hallucination. How could it be otherwise? Medical and psychiatric "science" are not interested in entertaining anything beyond that. They have to stay in lock step with the prevailing materialist paradigm, or else they risk being thought foolish and having their careers and reputations damaged. There is also big money behind the medicalization of human experience.

Is it any wonder that skeptical materialists embrace this "consensus" explanation for ADCs? Silly people, you're just seeing things! The experts say so.

Do you hear how patronizing that sounds? If you say ADCs are nothing but hallucination, you are saying that all the people reporting ADCs are so emotionally overwhelmed that they cannot distinguish reality from fantasy. You are saying they are so emotionally disturbed that they concoct a hallucination, just to make themselves feel better. Maybe they need some psychiatric medication, poor dears.

This pseudo-explanation ("grief-induced hallucination") is based completely on assumption, on faith. There is zero evidence that ADCs are the result of "chemical reactions or other abnormalities in the brain." Nothing at all. Don't be fooled into thinking this is science, just because the people saying it have white coats and clipboards. This is nothing more than a faith-based assumption, the faith rooted in a materialist worldview.

Materialism is the dominant worldview of science, medicine, and psychiatry. If that is your starting assumption, you *must* assume that ADCs are hallucinations. There is no alternative. That is why ADCs are defined from the start as hallucinatory; from that worldview, they cannot be anything other than that. But this is nothing more than an assumption. Again, there is zero evidence that ADCs are the result of "chemical reactions and/or abnormalities in the brain." And can you be less specific?

If that's not bad enough, the "grief-induced hallucination" theory rests on a further assumption – that the brain has a subconscious process which transforms grief into hallucination. How could you demonstrate such a subconscious process? You cannot. It is just another assumption, hidden behind medicalized terms such as "brain chemicals" and "abnormality." Give me a break.

Unless we have evidence that people reporting ADCs are *also*, at the same time, suffering from major mental disorders (e.g., severe depression, bipolar, psychotic disorders, drug intoxication), then it is arbitrary, narrow-minded, and insulting to dismiss those reports as nothing more than hallucinations.

Aside from those problems, there are also many ADC cases that run counter to this "grief-induced hallucination" theory. Let's turn to those.

Cases with Additional Corroboration

Earlier, we looked at simple visual ADC encounters. Let's talk now about reports that are not so simple – reports that contain features that lend them additional credibility. There are many such cases in the general ADC literature, but we will focus only on those related to animals. We will further confine ourselves only to the material I found in the published literature, excluding reports on the internet.

Of the 112 visual ADCs I found in the published literature, 63% of them were not "simple encounters" but instead contained additional features that help to support their credibility.

I categorized them as follows:

- o Multiple witness reports (19)

- o DKD (didn't know they were dead) reports (21)

- o No emotional attachment (12)

- o "Rescue" reports (5)

- o Appearances to skeptics (5)

- o Human ADC coincides with strange reaction of a living animal (6)

- o Physical events in the immediate environment that corresponded to what was being seen (1)

Many of these cases involved multiple sightings of the same animal over an extended period. I wanted to keep my counts conservative, so I counted multiple experiences by the same individual as a single ADC.

I will discuss each of these types and provide examples.

––––––––––––

Multiple Witnesses

I found 19 cases where there were multiple witnesses to the visual ADC of an animal. That is, the "deceased" animal appeared to two or more people, either at the same time or at different times.

Hardcore skeptics casually brush off a single person's ADC report. "She was just hallucinating, poor dear." It gets harder when there are two or more people involved. Are they both hallucinating? Both so overcome with grief that they lose touch with reality? Or is the first hallucinating and the second one just lying?

Here are two examples of multiple witness accounts.

Coco

Scott Smith relayed this account. Betty Smith of Manitoba had a dog named Coco. Betty said that someone threw a baited, poisoned bone in their yard, and Coco ate it. Coco became extremely sick, and Betty had to euthanize her.

A couple of days later, Betty saw Coco curled up in her favorite chair. Betty said, "She looked at me and then just disappeared. It was very clear." That is a simple encounter so far, similar to what many other people report.

However, her mother, who lived in the same house, also reported seeing the dog. The mother said she saw Coco running around the bed, then felt her curl up behind her, just like Coco would do when she was alive. That would be both a visual and tactile ADC.

There was also a third witness. One day, Betty walked across the street to her sister's home. A friend of her sister's, who had never seen Coco alive, insisted that she had seen a dog fitting Coco's description following Betty across the street.[6]

So, we have two people reporting ADCs of Coco, and a third person who had never met Coco, giving an accurate description of the dog, saying she saw it trailing Betty after its death.

Are all three of them hallucinating? Are all three of them so consumed by grief that they have lost touch with reality? That doesn't make sense. The third person didn't even know Coco, so she can't be having grief. There is no reason to make the arbitrary assumption that Betty and her mother are both so emotionally disturbed that they are subconsciously inventing a hallucination to make themselves feel better.

Penn

The second example comes from Vincent and Margaret Gaddis. They relate an account from Bayard Vellier. Mr. Vellier had to euthanize his dog, Penn. He buried Penn in the back garden. "Now," Vellier said, "here is the part I don't expect anyone to believe."

> *Weary from emotional strain, Vellier had gone to bed early. At three o'clock, he was awakened by the sound of Penn barking. It was 'gay, boisterous, excited.' He got up and went outside. Clearly visible in the bright moonlight, racing down a hill behind the house to the garden, came Penn – tail wagging, energetic and carefree as a puppy. He ran through the garden and around the lawn several times, then vanished.*

> *"The dog was unmistakably Penn," said Veiller. He added that he himself is not superstitious nor given to imagining things that don't exist, nor has he ever thought much about a hereafter. "I can't explain this, and it wasn't a dream. But I'll take my oath that he came back."*

> *The next morning, before Veiller could tell his wife about his experience, she told him she had heard*

Penn barking during the night and had gone to the window. There she too had seen him romping gaily about the garden and across the lawn until he disappeared.[7]

Did the husband and wife hallucinate the same thing? Separately? On the same night? That doesn't make any sense. That's not how hallucinations work. Note that Vellier's wife told him about her experience *before* he had shared his, so her report was not contaminated by his; she did not know about his experience before reporting her own.

Even if we indulge the hardcore skeptic and arbitrarily assume that Veiller was so consumed by grief that he hallucinated his dead dog romping in the garden, why would his wife have that *same hallucination*, on the same night, separately?

That is a sample of multiple witness ADCs accounts involving animals. There are many more. If you would like to read them, check out some of the sources in the notes.

––––––––––––

Didn't Know They Were Dead

Sometimes, a person will see a deceased animal that they did not realize was deceased at the time, only later learning about it. I call these DKD cases ("didn't know they were dead"). I found 21 of them in the literature, and I'm sure there are more out there.

These cases help to refute the materialist assumption that ADCs are merely grief-induced hallucinations. If you don't know the animal is dead, why would you hallucinate it in phantom form? Furthermore, you wouldn't be grieving the animal's death, because you don't it has died.

Here are two examples.

Judy

Mary Bagot lived in England, but she was vacationing at a hotel in France. Before leaving England, she had left Judy, her terrier, at home in the care of the gardener.

Sitting in the dining room of the hotel [in France], Mrs. Bagot suddenly saw her dog run across the floor. Unthinkingly, she exclaimed, 'Why, there's Judy!" There was no dog in the hotel. When Mrs. Bagot went upstairs to see her daughter, she told her of the experience.

A few days later, she received a letter telling her that Judy had been suddenly taken ill and had since died. The dog had been quite well, even on the morning of her death.[8]

Mrs. Bagot sees her "dead" dog, even though she has no idea the dog has died, and no reason to even suspect it might die. Mrs. Bagot's daughter provided further corroboration in the form of a diary entry made the day her mother told her about seeing Judy:

> *I distinctly remember my father and mother and sister and my cousin coming into my bedroom and all laughing and telling me how my mother had seen Judy running across the room. My mother was so positive about it that one of the others (I think my father) had asked the waiter if there were any dogs in the hotel, and he had answered in the negative.*

This corroborates Mrs. Bagot's account. Her daughter made that diary entry several days before they learned of Judy's death, which she also recorded in her diary.

———————

Bounce

This is a rather touching account from Anne Grazebrook, a woman in England. Anne had a sister who lived on an estate in the English countryside. Occasionally, Anne would visit her sister. On her sister's estate were a set of pure pedigree dogs, which the family owned and prized very much.

The family also had a dog named Bounce. Bounce was a stray they had taken in. Bounce was a mutt, not one of the pure pedigrees. Anne said, "Bounce received very little attention and petting, since he was an ugly, common-looking animal, in harsh contrast to the beautiful pedigreed dogs belonging to the family." She said that Bounce seemed to feel inferior, and she felt sorry for him. She tried to extend kindness to him when she would visit. As a result, Bounce developed an affectionate attachment to Anne.

Sometime later, while Anne was staying with friends in Aberdeen, she was awakened about 5 a.m. by the barking of a dog in her bedroom. She reported the following:

> "I sat up in bed, and to my surprise, I saw Bounce. I put out my hand and felt him. He had his collar on, and he was warm and solid to the touch.'
>
> "In utter astonishment, I exclaimed, 'Bounce, how did you get here?' and a human voice replied, 'I was shot yesterday. I have come to say goodbye!'
>
> "Then the dog was gone. How he came, how he went, whence came the voice, I could not say. I was left in a state of complete bewilderment."[9]

I'll bet. Weeks later, Anne got a letter from her sister's governess. The governess explained that "as the family was going away, and as it was impossible to find a home for a mongrel like Bounce, it was thought kinder to have him shot." Bounce was shot on the afternoon of August 24. He had appeared in Anne's bedroom 5 a.m. the following morning, saying he had been shot yesterday.

> "I can only add," Anne said, "that at the time when I saw the dog, it did not occur to me even remotely that he was dead. His bark was loud enough to rouse me from a heavy sleep. He did not look distressed, merely excited as a dog might be at the sight of an old friend. And I can only repeat that when I patted him, he was apparently alive and tangible beneath my hand."

The authors add:

> With whatever means Bounce crossed the great abyss, it is touching that this lonely but affectionate dog, shot because of his ancestry and lack of beauty, should at death express gratitude for the only love that had ever been shown to him.[9]

You cannot explain these sorts of cases as grief-induced hallucinations. These people have no idea that the animal has died; they don't even know the animal is sick or in any danger of dying. Even if you assume that the brain subconsciously concocts hallucinations to make itself feel better, these people's brains have no such need. They don't know the animal is dead. They have no grief. And yet the deceased animal appears to them, shortly after it has died – and in this case, even tells her how he was killed and when.

Those are two examples, but there are many more, both in the general ADC and animal literature. See the sources for other accounts.

———————

No Emotional Attachment

Some people see "deceased" animals to whom they have no emotional attachment. To be sure, these are the exception: most ADCs occur with animals to whom we are emotionally bonded. But sometimes, there are ADCs involving animals to whom no real emotional connection exists.

These cases cannot be explained away as grief-induced hallucinations, either. The person is not grieving.

I found 12 such cases. Here is one example.

Mary Seiler was working at an architectural company in San Diego. One morning, she walked through the drafting department, because she needed to make some photocopies. The department was well-lit and full of people. As she passed by one of the drafting tables, something caught her eye.

> *"I looked down and to my surprise, I saw a gray cat with yellow eyes materialize. It leaped up and rubbed itself against the legs of the draftsman, who seemed oblivious, then disappeared. I was shocked! I was alert and observant and noticed that the cat seemed to lack depth but had width and breadth."*[10]

Mary approached the man at the drafting table. She asked him whether he owned a cat. The man replied yes, but the cat had been killed two weeks earlier – run over by a car in the street.

Mary told the man what she had seen. The man then confirmed that Mary's description matched his own cat, the one who had died. He thanked her for telling him. He mentioned to Mary that "he had felt the felt the cat's presence many times before, but he thought he was imagining things."

If ADCs are merely grief-fueled hallucinations, why would Mary hallucinate a stranger's cat, in the middle of a busy office, while preoccupied with making photocopies? She is not in grief. She doesn't even know the man or his cat. She has no need to subconsciously concoct a comforting hallucination for herself, nor would such a hallucination be comforting anyway. These skeptical "explanations" just do not hold up.

See the source material if you would like to read other, similar cases.

––––––––––––

"Rescue" ADCs

Another type of case that helps to refute skeptical counter-claims is what I'll call a "rescue" ADC. In these cases, the timing of the ADC is the key. The ADC is timed in such a way that it seems to warn a person of danger and allows him/her to escape that danger.

Here is an example.

Robin Deland had a dog named Jeff. Deland had rescued Jeff from dire straits as a young dog. Jeff passed away six months prior to the event described below. Deland was driving alone at night along a narrow, winding dirt road in the Colorado mountains.

> *Deland had started up a sharp incline when suddenly a dog appeared in his headlights, only a short distance ahead in the road. The animal stood there unmoving and Deland had to break to a stop. He sat frozen in his seat, because the dog, now only a few feet away and clearly detailed in his car lights, was Jeff.*

They were extremely close. Deland knew every hair on the dog's body, and Jeff was extremely large for his breed. He had a massive head but a somewhat short nose for a collie. Deland is quite certain that his rendezvous on a rocky mountain precipice was with Jeff, even though the dog had died six months prior. [11]

Deland felt "awed and bewildered." He got out of his car, attempting to reach Jeff. However, as he walked toward the dog and tried to touch him, Jeff turned around and walked up the road toward the peak of the incline. Deland followed.

He topped the incline, and just beyond, silhouetted by the moonlight, was a massive rock slide, burying the road. If his car had reached that point, it would have been certain death. There would have been no way he could have kept from plunging off the cliff in a drop of several hundred feet.

Deland stood there for several long minutes, staring at the rock slide and the depths below. He was shaken. He looked around for Jeff, but there was no sign of him. Deland had no doubt that it was Jeff he saw. He is also convinced, that, were it not for Jeff's appearance, he would have died. Deland had saved Jeff's life many years before, and he is convinced that Jeff came back to return the favor.

The author adds: "Hallucination? If Deland is hallucinating, isn't it rather strange that the nonexistent Jeff so appropriately saved his life?" Strange indeed.

This is another instance where the "grief-induced hallucination" theory flops. Apart from the timing of the "hallucination," there was no grief to induce a hallucination in the first place. Jeff had died six months earlier. Presumably, any intense grief had passed by then. Deland was not thinking about Jeff; he was focused on the road.

To be sure, these cases are rare. I only found 5 in the literature. Nevertheless, they provide additional evidence that something real is going on here, which cannot be brushed off as a hallucination.

————————

Appearances to Skeptics

I found five cases in which animals appear in visual ADCs to skeptics – to people who have no belief in an afterlife. These people typically consider afterlife beliefs "woo-woo" nonsense.

Why would someone who does not believe in an afterlife subconsciously concoct a hallucination that contradicts their worldview? Our worldviews are very important to us; they ground us in a feeling of security and knowing. We have cognitive biases that help anchor them in place (e.g., confirmation bias). We know from neuroimaging studies that when our worldview gets threatened, our amygdala gets activated. The amygdala is the part of our brain which processes primitive emotions like fear and anger, as well as threats to survival.[12]

The "grief-induced hallucination" theory assumes that the hallucination makes you feel better. But an ADC would disturb a skeptic, because it would contradict his/her basic worldview. Why would a skeptic subconsciously concoct a hallucination that would be upsetting and disturbing?

Here is an example of such a case.

Barbara Meyers had a white poodle named Skila. Barbara had been seeing a chiropractor for many years. When Skila developed spinal problems, Barbara asked her chiropractor to work on Skila. The chiropractor said no – he only worked on people, not animals. Besides, he wasn't much of an animal person. He had never owned a dog or any other animal; he had never even petted a dog. Barbara persisted, though, and eventually, the chiropractor relented. He reluctantly agreed to work on Skila. Barbara described the chiropractor as "a true skeptic – more than a skeptic, in fact," about the afterlife.

The chiropractic treatment seemed to help Skila a great deal. Barbara said:

"It was just marvelous. He would do the adjustment, and she would go rickshaw all around the office, run down the hallway outside the exam room and run back and jump into his arms with an obvious, "Thanks a lot!" He always knew when we were there even before we were in, because he could hear her coming down that hall. She would always go down the hall and look for him."

Skila eventually passed away. About six months later, Barbara received "a very agitated" phone call from the chiropractor.

"He told me the following: He was in his office at the end of the at the end of the building, working at his desk, and there were a few patients waiting out front and the secretary. He heard something in the hallway. It wasn't the footsteps of his secretary or patients coming down.

"He was compelled to get up, and when he got up and peeked out his office door, Skila was walking down the hallway as she had done so many times before. It was not a feeling or an image or some kind of shadowy sensation. It was what is known as a solid visitation. He was stunned."

Most people who see visual ADCs are comforted by the appearance. Not this skeptic:

> *"He called me, not so much to tell me that Skila had come to visit him, but because he thought he was having a breakdown. You see, he was a person (since I knew him for so many years and we talked about many things) believed that all of this "stuff," as he would call it, was simply the effect of a grief-stricken mind. But that day, everything changed for him."*[13]

She adds that he had the same experience several days later. "He was so upset; it was really a frightening experience for him." She said he thought he was having a "mental breakdown."

Like many skeptics, the chiropractor had dismissed ADC reports as "simply the effect of a grief-stricken mind." But then he has an experience of his own. He is not in grief. The dog has been dead for six months. It wasn't his dog. He has no belief in an afterlife at all. He did not find the "hallucination" comforting at all. In fact, it was the opposite – he found it frightening and upsetting, because it upended his worldview. He thought he was going crazy. If visual ADCs are nothing more than grief-induced hallucinations, why would he have one? He has no grief to alleviate. The experience was frightening, not comforting.

The chiropractor was so emotionally impacted by these events that he adopted a dog. The dog became the love of his life, and "when she was diagnosed with cancer, how he cried. What he wouldn't have done and did do for her. And this was the man who had never patted a dog on the head."

Other accounts of skeptics encountering visual ADCs of animals can be found in the sources.

———————

Coinciding Animal Reactions

I found half a dozen cases in which an animal reacts strangely at the same time the human being is experiencing a visual animal ADC. These cases add some corroboration to the human report. I don't want to overstate things, because we cannot know what the animal is experiencing. Yet, the animal does seem to be reacting to something unusual in the environment, which suggests that the ADC is not simply a subjective, internal experience.

Here is one example. Dee Dee Mascetti of Burbank, California, had to euthanize her cat, Shrimpie. A year later, she was watching TV with her two other cats, Guy and PJ. Dee Dee stated:

"I looked over and saw Shrimpie exiting the kitchen. Guy and PJ both sat up suddenly and, with hair standing on end, watched intently as Shrimpie walked along the wall of the living room to the second bedroom. As we watched, Shrimpie walked through the closed door of the second bedroom."

Guy and PJ ran to the door to sniff, but when Dee Dee opened it, the two cats "ran like hell in the other direction, and it took them a while before they would enter than room again."[14]

Dee Dee is having a visual ADC, and, at the same time, the two cats seem to be reacting to the same thing. They both become suddenly vigilant ("hair standing on end") at the same time, and their gaze seems to follow what Dee Dee is looking at. The cats sniff at the door where Dee Dee saw Shrimpie disappear. And then the cats "run like hell" when the door is opened.

I would consider that a multiple witness account, except that the other witnesses are cats, and cats can't give us verbal reports. But it helps corroborate Dee Dee's story. I would add that grief also is not in play here. A year has gone by since Shrimpie's death.

That is one example. I found half a dozen of these cases, in which the animal's reaction helped to corroborate the human report.

Coinciding Physical Movement

There was one case in which a woman reported a physical change in the environment that corresponded to a visual ADC.

A woman by the name of Katherine had a cat named Demi. Demi passed away. Katherine was devastated. She reported:

> *"As I was lying on my bed, halfway between sleep and consciousness, something caught my eye, or so I thought. I looked over toward the bookcase where Demi loved to climb. In my state of grief and grogginess, I simply thought that I had imagined the black blur as it moved down from the bookcase [...]."*

> *"Something made me fully wake up and look up to her favorite shelf, where I had the three pictures. When I did, I knew I had not imagined that black blur, because every one of those pictures had been knocked over, exactly as she had done many times during her life."*

Katherine explained that, when Demi was alive, she would often climb that bookcase and would knock over those same three pictures. Katherine had a visual ADC, and she found physical changes in the environment that corresponded to her ADC. These physical changes corresponded to the cat's typical behavior when alive. The physical changes lend some additional corroboration to her report.

I only found one case like this in the visual ADC literature for animals. However, there are other cases like it in the human ADC literature.[15]

––––––––––

Visual ADC Wrap Up

To sum up, then, I found 112 published reports of visual ADCs of animals. Of these, 37% were simple encounters and 63% had additional corroborative evidence. More specifically, there were 19 multiple witness accounts, 21 DKD accounts, 12 reports where there was no emotional connection, 5 rescue ADCs, 5 encounters by skeptic/non-believers, and some other types. Note, these are just ADCs of the visual sort; we'll cover auditory, tactile, and olfactory ADCs in a later chapter.

In addition to the published reports reviewed here, there were also 280 animal ADCs on adcrf.org and hundreds more posted elsewhere on the internet. I did not have the wherewithal to search for and include them all, but they testify to the widespread nature of animals appearing after "death."

"Grief-induced hallucination" does not hold up as an explanation for these ADCs. It is based on arbitrary assumptions, unsupported by evidence, and is patronizing to those who have these experiences. It also completely fails to account for the majority of evidence reviewed in this chapter, to say nothing of the broader literature.

Chapter 5

DO ANIMALS QUALIFY FOR

THE AFTERLIFE?

Let's take a break from reviewing evidence and look at the subject from a different angle – a theological one. Are animals allowed through the pearly gates? Do they qualify for an afterlife? Many people think they do not. As I'll show below, about 27% of people in the United States believe that human beings qualify for an afterlife, but animals do not.

Polling Data

In 2021, Pew Research found that 83% of people believe in an afterlife of some sort, and 17% do not.[1] Of those who responded to the poll, 75% said they believed in "heaven and/or hell" – usually both, but sometimes just heaven. One percent said they only believed in hell, not heaven (I don't think I want to meet those people.) Seven percent said they believed in an afterlife, but "not necessarily in terms of heaven and hell."

That poll was taken in the United States, so it won't generalize to other countries. An IPSOS global survey of 23 countries and 18,829 adults showed that 51% of people believed in an afterlife of some sort.[2] Among those who believe in an afterlife, roughly half believe that "you go to heaven or hell." The other half believe in an afterlife of some sort, "but not specifically in a heaven or hell." I belong to the latter camp.

Globally, then, 49% of people do not believe in animal afterlife, because they do not believe in any sort of afterlife. In the US, the percentage of disbelievers in the afterlife is much lower (17%). But the number of disbelievers in animal afterlife is higher than that, because some of those who *do* believe in an afterlife only believe human beings qualify.

How many people believe that humans have an afterlife but animals do not? Figuring that out is harder, because few pollsters ask specifically about belief in animal afterlife. Neither IPSOS or Pew did.

I did find one poll that asked the question, though. It was taken in the United States, so it won't necessarily generalize beyond that, but it was all I found. Three professors at North Carolina State University asked 800 people about their belief in animal afterlife. They found that, among those who believed in an afterlife for people, 73% also believed in an afterlife for animals. The other 27% did not – they thought only human beings qualified for an afterlife; animals did not.[3]

To estimate the total percentage of those who believe in animal afterlife (at least in the US), we can combine that result with the Pew Research poll. The result suggests that about 60% of people in the US believe in animal afterlife, and 40% do not. Of the 40% who do not, some disbelieve in any sort of afterlife, and some believe in an afterlife but think that only people "get in."

Of course, we cannot decide whether animals have an afterlife by consulting poll results. It isn't a popularity contest. Either animals have an afterlife, or they don't. But still, I think it's interesting to see how many people believe that only human beings qualify for an afterlife, not animals. In the US, it's about 27%.

Why do these people think that only human beings qualify but not animals? We don't have poll data on that question, but I can answer it pretty easily. It's because of religious beliefs. More specifically, members of the more conservative, fundamentalist wings of Christianity are likely to hold this belief. I'll say more about that in the next section.

Christian Beliefs

The relationship between Christianity and animals is a complex one. I will be talking here only about Christian views of animal afterlife.

During the thousands of years of Christian history, many Christian theologians have posited that only human beings are "made in the image of God," and so only people get admitted through the pearly gates. Animals do not; they return to dust.

Animals do not have immortal souls, and so they do not qualify for the afterlife.

There is no "official" Christian position on this question – in part, that is because there is no "official" Christianity. Instead, there are hundreds of different Christian denominations in the US alone and tens of thousands globally. Beliefs about animal afterlife will vary, depending on the denomination and the church.

In most cases, the beliefs are not formally encoded as official doctrine of the church, but instead are conveyed through other, less formal, teachings. Even when the church itself does not take an official position, theologians and preachers representing that church do take one.

For instance, although the Catholic church does not have an official position on the matter, one of its most influential theologians, Thomas Aquinas, argued that only human beings were "made in the image of God" – animals were not – and therefore, only humans had an afterlife; animals did not. Aquinas was not saying something new, but he articulated it decisively, and his views were highly influential, shaping the church for centuries; his influence can still be felt today.

I will not attempt to convey all of Aquinas' argument, but I want to focus on his idea that only human beings have reason and moral sense. Aquinas thought that these were fundamental attributes of God. In that sense, humans were "made in the image of God." Only human beings possessed these characteristics; animals did not have reason or conscience, and therefore they were not "made in the image of God." They did not qualify to be with God in the afterlife, because they did not share in His nature.

If you see the world that way – divided into humans and animals, with one possessing reason and moral sense, and the other lacking it – then it makes sense. Only human beings share in God's nature, so only human beings are fit to hang out with God in heaven. This argument shaped the beliefs of Christians worldwide for centuries.

Times have changed, though. Aquinas was writing in the 13th century. Many Christians today – 73% in the US – believe that both human beings and animals are welcome into "heaven." However, 27% are not. I suspect most of these are in the conservative, fundamentalist camp.

If you are one of these people, you might check out some books that argue for animal afterlife from a Bible-based perspective. There are many (e.g., *Cold Noses at the Pearly Gates*, by Gary Kurz).

I won't be taking that tack, though. Instead, I want to focus on Aquinas' supposition that animals lack reason and moral sense. That seems to be the theological fulcrum on which he denies animal afterlife. Forgive my simplification, but the argument goes something like this:

1. The only creatures suitable to exist with God in heaven are those who share in his fundamental nature.

2. Reason and moral sense are fundamental attributes of God.

3. Human beings have reason and moral sense. They share God's fundamental nature, and therefore, they are suited to be with God in heaven.

4. Animals, however, lack these attributes. They lack reason and moral sense. Therefore, they are not suitable to be with God in heaven. They are returned to dust.

I don't agree with the first premise. I don't think the afterlife is that simple; it is much more multi-faced than that. However, making that case would take us far afield. We'll let that one go for now.

I will focus instead on premise #4, the assertion that animals lack reason and moral sense. That is what I want to challenge. If that premise is wrong, and I'm going to argue it is, then the rationale for excluding animals from the afterlife falls apart.

Reason

Reason is the capacity to engage in thought, especially abstract thought. There is no doubt that human beings have cognitive abilities that dwarf that of other species. Our culture and civilization would not exist without it.

Aquinas was heavily influenced by Aristotle, who described human beings as "the rational animal." Aristotle drew a sharp distinction between humans and animals in that regard. Animals do not think, he said – they are creatures of instinct and reflex. Only human beings use reason.

Aquinas adopted Aristotle's bifurcation between man and animal. Because of that, this distinction between people and animals, based on rationality, was driven deep into Christian belief. That is not the only reason, but it was an important one.

Clearly, our ability to reason vastly outstrips those of other animals. However, that does not mean animals completely lack the ability to reason. If we say that, we have fallen into binary, dichotomous thinking, as if species came in only two types: rational and irrational, with no mixture and no gradient.

Over the past 30 or 40 years, animal cognition research has repeatedly demonstrated that many animals have the capacity to reason.[4] Our primate cousins – chimpanzees, gorillas, bonobos, etc. – demonstrate the capacity for reason. Wolves and dogs show the ability to reason. So do birds and mice. Dolphins and whales are highly intelligent. Even alligators and crocodiles show rudimentary forms of reason.

To be clear, that doesn't mean gorillas are doing differential calculus, or that goats are writing philosophy dissertations. The reasoning abilities we are talking about are elementary; for example:

- classifying and categorizing objects
- learning from their own mistakes
- learning from observing others' mistakes
- constructing and using tools.

It is true that these abilities are simple enough. But they do represent forms of reasoning. If animals lacked the capacity for thought – if they were just collections of instinct, primitive emotion, and reflex (as Aristotle and Aquinas thought) – they could not perform them.

That is not all. Animal cognition research also demonstrates that many animals think ahead, contemplate the future, and anticipate potential consequences. These are forms of reasoning as well. It is a cliché to admire animals for their ability to live in the present moment, but in fact, that is not necessarily where they are all the time. They think about the future. They anticipate or dread what might happen. They start, modify, or stop behavior depending on their consideration of consequences. This is not mere reflex; it requires thought.

Some animals even demonstrate higher-level cognitive abilities, including self-awareness and a sense of personal identity. Self-awareness was once thought to be a uniquely human attribute. However, chimpanzees, dolphins, elephants, and even dogs (when tested properly) all demonstrate self-awareness. Not only does that show advanced cognitive function, it implies a sense of personal identity.

Animals also use language, of course. Decades ago, we thought that only human beings used language, but that is clearly not the case. Human beings do have a linguistic superpower -- abstract, symbolic, written language – which does not appear in any other animal. Nonetheless, many animals possess complex and sophisticated forms of language. Animal languages are widespread. Many of these languages are complex and intricate, and we are only beginning to decode them.

We also need to have some intellectual humility in this area. There is a danger of anthropocentrism. When assessing animals' cognitive abilities, we have too often used our own abilities as the yardstick. The famous biologist and animal researcher Frans De Waal explains this in his book, *Are We Smart Enough to Know How Smart Animals Are.*

De Wall gives example after example, illustrating that animals' so-called "failures" on intelligence tests have often been our own failures to adapt our evaluations to their modes of thought. We were evaluating animal intelligence using our standards, our preferred modes of thought. When researchers finally recognized their anthropocentrism and adapted their evaluation to the animal's preferred modes of thought, lo and behold, it turned out that animals are actually pretty smart. They are just smart in their own ways, not in ours.[5]

Certainly, human beings have intellectual capacities that far outstrip those of animals. But animals are smart in their own ways. They are smart in the ways they need to be smart. A cat is smart in the ways a cat needs to be smart; a rat is smart in the ways a rat needs to be smart.

In sum, then, animal cognition research makes it quite clear that animals have the capacity for reason. This capacity shows up in basic ways across a wide range of species and in advanced forms in some others.

We should not conceive of reasoning as either being present or absent. To do so is to fall prey to the simplest of cognitive errors: all-or-nothing thinking (also known as black-and-white, binary, or dichotomous thinking). Reason is not an all-or-nothing thing. It exists on a continuum – or perhaps "spectrum" would be a better word. Human beings excel in some areas, but that hardly means animals lack the ability to reason – that they are merely a mindless collection of instinct and reflexes. That picture does not do them justice at all.

It is time that we set aside outdated, simplistic, all-or-nothing modes of conceptualizing this issue of reason. If human beings are truly the "rational animal," we can do better than that.

―――――――――

Morality

Through most of history, animals have been considered amoral, i.e., without moral sense. They do not (so the story goes) have any free will – their actions are just the result of instinct, feeling, and reflex. There is no thought involved, and certainly no moral sensibility. The categories of "right and wrong" simply do not apply to them.

Human beings, however, have a moral sense. It is the thing inside us (some call it conscience) that lets us know when an action is right or wrong. Animals, it was thought, lacked this moral sense. That was the second reason to eject them from the afterlife – God had a moral sense, but animals did not; they were not "made in the image of God," and thus, they did not qualify for heaven.

But is that true? Do animals lack moral sense?

This is a trickier question, in part because questions of "morality" in animals are difficult to investigate. The research is not as robust here as it is in animal cognition.

However, there is research suggesting that animals have the fundamental building blocks of a moral sense. I'll describe that research briefly.

Empathy and Care

Animal research has repeatedly demonstrated that most mammals and some birds exhibit empathy.[6] Empathy is the ability to understand what the other being is experiencing – to put yourself in their paws, so to speak.

Although the relationship between empathy and morality is complex, empathy is bound up with moral behavior; it functions as one of its core motivators. The aim of moral behavior is often to reduce others' suffering, and empathy enables us to see that suffering. If we don't "feel with" the sufferer, then we will often not be motivated to relieve their suffering. Sociopaths, who lack empathy, are not known for their charity work.

To be sure, empathy does not *always* lead to helping behavior. Sometimes it leads to the opposite, as when empathy for our in-group blinds us to the suffering of the out-group.[7] But in many situations, empathy is correlated with compassion for others' suffering and motivates helping behavior.

If empathy is a core motivator of moral behavior, and if many animals exhibit empathy, it is too much to say that animals have at least *some* moral sense? I don't think so.

In addition, we can look at the many examples of animals caring for each other, working together, and extending kindness to each other. Members of an animal group will help each other, groom each other, offer food to each other, play with each other, and fight off threats to protect each other.

When we see these behaviors in human beings, we recognize them as "good" (i.e., as moral). However, when we see these behaviors in animals, we (or at least researchers) often dismiss them as nothing more than evolutionary adaptations that aid in survival. Even if these behaviors *are* evolutionarily advantageous (which can be a difficult case to make), that does not mean they are amoral, i.e., that they arise strictly as automatic reflex, without any moral sense – unless you want to say the same of our species: that our helping, protecting, and caring behaviors are amoral, without moral sense.

Just because a behavior is evolved does not mean it is amoral. A behavior can be both evolved and moral; there is no necessary contradiction there.

Furthermore, some animals extend empathy and care to *other species* – so-called cross-species altruism. Animals will sometimes rescue members of other species from danger. Animals will sometimes adopt orphans of other species. They may befriend members of other species, share food with them, and play with them. They will help warn other species of danger, sometimes fighting off a threat, even saving their lives.

Evolutionary biologists stretch and strain credulity to explain cross-species altruism as a mere evolutionary adaptation, designed to increase the odds of survival. It is not clear to me why cross-species altruism, which involves spending precious energy and resources, even risking your life in some cases, to help a member of another species, would promote individual survival.

There is an anthropocentrism at play here again. When we see that behavior in humans – extending care to other species – we clearly recognize that as "good," as admirable. A while back, I saw a video of men working to rescue an elephant calf from a pit into which it had fallen. I instinctively recognized that as a "good" act, and I applauded those men. Why can we not recognize goodness when an animal does it?

Animals show empathy and compassion in other ways as well. Elephants and other mammals show compassion and concern towards others who are suffering or experiencing grief; they console each other. Animals offer aid to each other. They build relationships of trust. And we see evidence of "pay it forward" behavior, even in rats. [8]

If animals demonstrate empathy and compassion for others, is that not part of what we mean by having a moral sense?

I am not arguing that animals show as much cross-species altruism as human beings do. They don't. Nor am I arguing that animals are as influenced by moral or ethical considerations as human beings are. They clearly are not. However, I am arguing that animals behave in ways that we would recognize as "good" in our own species. They exhibit empathy, care, and kindness – not only to members of their own species, but sometimes to members of other species. That is evidence that they have some of the fundamental elements of a moral sensibility.

Fairness

Concerns with fairness or justice are central to our notion of morality. To many people's surprise, animal research suggests that animals may have a sense of fairness and justice – rudimentary, to be sure, but present. This shows up in a variety of ways. For example:

- o Animals have implicit rules about sharing and equity.
- o Animals have rules about fair play; if those rules are broken, they become upset.
- o Animals value honesty.

- o Animals value social reciprocity.
- o Animals have codes governing forgiveness.[9]

Animals, then, seem to have a sense of fairness. That is not to say animals always behave fairly. Neither do human beings. But animals do have what we would recognize as "moral" codes – rules about right and wrong behavior. And for the most part, they abide by them. For instance, despite the stereotypes about aggressive chimps, studies have shown that 93% of primate interactions are positive and prosocial.

I don't want to be misunderstood. I'm not claiming that animals' sense of justice is on the same level as our own. I'm not saying we should nominate a monkey to the Supreme Court. I'm simply saying that many animals exhibit a sense of fairness or justice. And a sense of fairness or justice is a fundamental aspect of morality.

In fact, if you accept the evolutionary theory as is, where would human beings get their morality, if not through the evolutionary process – and so, why wouldn't some animals also possess such attributes?

Animals, then, have core elements of what we would call a moral sense. They exhibit empathy and compassion, which commonly undergird moral behavior. They show empathy, care, and concern for members of their own group. Sometimes, they even demonstrate cross-species altruism. Many animals also exhibit a sense of fairness or justice, which are core features of moral behavior.

I don't want to overstate the case. Human beings are vastly more concerned with moral behavior than animals are, and our moral sense is much better developed. However, that does not mean animals *lack* a moral sense entirely. Animal research suggests that they indeed possess some of the fundamental constituents of moral sense. Their moral sense is simpler and more rudimentary, but it exists. Indeed, from an evolutionary angle, it would be hard to explain why humans have a moral sense, if the building blocks did not already exist in the animal kingdom.

Again, we need to avoid thinking in simplistic binaries, as if moral sense was either present or absent. Moral sense, like almost any other attribute you care to name, exists on a continuum, not in an all-or-nothing fashion. Yes, human beings have a much more advanced moral code, but animals have one, too, albeit at a lower level. Moral sense exists on a spectrum.

And again, we should have some humility. Human beings may have a better developed moral sense than animals, but human beings are also the source of more suffering and death on the planet than any other species, by far. Humans have a wonderful capacity for goodness, but let's not pat ourselves on the back too hard – we also have a tremendous capacity for cruelty and destruction. Human evil exists on scale unimaginable to animals. I will spare you the litany. If you want to assert that only human beings are "made in the image of God," then you've got some explaining to do.

In any event, animals have a moral sense. It may not be as complex and advanced as ours, but it is there.

————————

The Golden Rule

Religious denominations will often set up an afterlife demarcation. They decide who gets in, and who gets left out. Who goes to heaven, who goes to hell, and who gets dusted. If you examine these "who's in" and "who's out" decisions, you will notice something interesting. The group making the decisions always ends up "in," and the ones who are not on the committee end up "out." Funny how that works.

It reminds me of a comic I read when I was a kid, the Wizard of Id. The diminutive king said to his wayward knight that he believed in the golden rule. "Whoever has the gold makes the rules."

The people in charge make decisions in their own favor. No surprise there. But it applies to these afterlife discriminations, too. Christians ask themselves, "Who gets into heaven?" And their answer is, "Why, Christians, of course!" Go figure. I don't mean to pick on Christianity; it's just the religion I'm most familiar with. Many religions have their own version of this, couched in different language, but setting up similar demarcations between who is worthy and who is not.

Setting up those demarcations has several advantages. It helps to define your group identity. If you are a leader, it helps consolidates power, because your group will be more willing to support and fight for you. It justifies mistreating the outgroup. It also feeds our ego.

He who has the gold makes the rules; he who holds power, including religious authority, makes the decisions about who is "in" and who is "out." And they usually decide the question in their own favor and in favor of their group. This includes decisions about who gets an afterlife and who does not. And guess who wasn't invited to *that* meeting? How many dogs and cats do you suppose were sitting around *that* conference table?

I think this is part of how animals got excluded from the afterlife, at least among some religious denominations. Human beings asked themselves, "Who gets into heaven?" And human beings decided that human beings get in, and animals don't. Big surprise.

Fortunately, over the course of history, many of these lines of demarcation have softened. For instance, not too long ago, many Christians believed black people were not fully human and so did not go to heaven, whereas only a few backwards Christians believe that today. Same with gay people: a few decades ago, they were destined for eternal barbeque, but now most churches happily accept them. Sure, there is still some trailing residue, but the general trend is for these old discriminations to fall. The "we are in, you are out" judgments soften over time. Things change.

The same thing is happening with animals. Pope Francis was speaking with a young boy who wanted to know if his dog – who had died recently – was in heaven. "One day, we will see all of our animals again," the Pope replied. "Paradise is open to all of God's creatures." Good for him. I have heard many priests and pastors endorse a belief that animals are in "heaven." And many books have been published recently that support animal afterlife from a Biblical perspective.

I suspect this trend will continue. For those who believe in an afterlife, animals will increasingly be seen as a natural part of that picture.

————————

Conclusion

To return to where we started: some Christians (about 27% in the US) believe that only human beings have an afterlife, and animals do not. They exclude animals from the afterlife based on the notion that only people are "made in the image of God." In particular, only human beings share the Godly qualities of reason and moral sense. Since animals lack reason and moral sense (so the story goes), they are not entitled to hang out with God. They are not worthy of an afterlife.

I have described research that refutes that premise in multiple ways. Animals have the capacity for reason, and they also have a moral sense. Although those capacities are not nearly as well-developed as in humans, they exist nonetheless.

As a consequence, we have to reject the old, simplistic bifurcation between humans and animals. These capacities exist on a continuum, not as a simple binary. Animals have these capacities; and since they do, the premise (#4) that they lack them is false. But that premise was the rationale for excluding animals from the afterlife. If that premise is false, then the rationale for excluding animals falls apart, because that is what the exclusion was based on.

If any of those 27% are reading this, I encourage you to consider this argument. If animals possess the fundamentals of reason and moral sense, then they qualify for an afterlife.

Chapter 6

AUDITORY, TACTILE, AND

OLFACTORY ADCS

In visual ADCs, people "see Spot run," after he has died. But people not only see Spot run – they also hear, feel, and smell Spot, after he has died. These are auditory, tactile, and olfactory ADCs. I have yet to read about a gustatory ADC, someone tasting their dead pet. I'm thinking that's probably a good thing.

All totaled, I found 55 auditory, 42 tactile, and 6 olfactory ADCs in the published literature (103 total). As we saw in the chapter on visual ADCs, this is a significant underestimate of the number of actual ADC reports. There are hundreds of other reports scattered about on the internet (e.g., adcrf.org, pet loss, and afterlife forums). To retain my sanity, I confined myself to just the published accounts.

First, I will briefly describe some examples of how auditory, tactile, and olfactory ADCs manifest. Next, I will discuss simple encounters, followed by cases that have additional, corroborating factors.

Auditory ADCs

I found 55 auditory ADCs in the published literature. Here are some examples of how auditory ADCs may manifest, after an animal has died:

- The distinctive sound of their bark or meow
- A clinking of tags
- The characteristic click of toenails across wood flooring
- The sound of a tail whapping against the ground
- Distinctive whines or snores
- A scratching at the door

Here is an example of a simple auditory ADC:

Thomas Goheen of Fullerton, CA, reported that he heard his cat "meow" at 4 a.m.. The sound seemed to be coming from the hallway. Thomas said that this behavior was very characteristic of the cat. When she was alive, she would meow around 4 a.m. every morning, because she wanted to be let outside.[1]

This is what I termed a "simple encounter" earlier. Apart from Thomas's report of his experience, there are no other factors that might add to its credibility. We are left to either believe the account or write it off as misperception.

As with visual ADCs, there are many cases of auditory ADCs that are not so simple – they have additional factors lending them credibility. We will get to those shortly.

Tactile ADCs

I found 42 tactile ADCs in the literature. In a tactile ADCs, the person experiences a tactile, physical sensation associated with the animal, after it has passed. Here are some ways that may manifest:

- The physical sensation of the animal's body pressed up against you
- Feeling the animal rub up against their legs
- Feeling the sensation of their skin or fur
- Feeling them jump onto the bed, with the mattress seeming to depress
- Feeling the bed covers move

Here is one example of a simple tactile ADC.

Mary Peed of Georgia reported that she has felt a "kind of nudge" on the blanket over her knees, which matched what her dog, Tiffany, did when she was alive. She also reported feeling pressure against her leg when in bed, coming from the same corner where Tiffany would sleep.[2]

This is a simple encounter, and you are left to either take Mary at her word or write her off as mistaken or hallucinating. We will cover cases with corroborating factors below.

Olfactory ADCs

Compared to other types, olfactory animal ADCs are relatively rare. I found only 6 documented in the literature. I suspect that the lower frequency is due to the fact that humans' olfactory sense is not very well-developed, compared to our other senses. Our visual and auditory senses are dominant, so we get more reports of visual and auditory ADCs than olfactory ones. If dogs were reporting ADCs, we'd probably be getting a lot more olfactory reports.

In an olfactory ADC, people smell something that reminds them of their pet. They may smell the animal's characteristic scent, for instance, or perhaps a special shampoo they used to bathe them.

Here is an example.

Nicole Lockard of Maryland had a dalmatian named Patchouli, who passed away a few months prior to this experience. Nicole had a grandfather who passed away several years before that. Nicole said that, after his death, she would often smell her grandfather's very distinct scent, which she described as a mix of Chesapeake Bay air, tobacco, and Polo cologne.

Nicole reported the following:

> *"Since she was a puppy, I loved smelling Patchouli's paw pads. They kind of smelled like popcorn. Every so often, out of nowhere, I get that familiar whiff of my grandfather, followed by the smell of my Patchouli's paws. I like to think that they are taking care of each other somewhere and sending me a little 'hello.' They never met in life, but they would've been great friends. Maybe now they are."* [3]

Cases with Corroborating Factors

Roughly half of the 103 auditory, tactile, and olfactory ADCs were simple encounters. You either believe the person's report (as evidence of something supernatural) or else dismiss it as misperception, dishonesty, wishful thinking, or the like.

The other half of the cases, though, had factors that lent the report additional credibility. These cases clumped into the same categories we saw with visual ADCs:

o   Multiple witnesses

- o DKD cases – people experiencing an ADC of an animal they did not know was deceased
- o Cases where the person has no emotional attachment to the animal being perceived
- o "Rescue" ADCs, which seem to be timed in such a way as to warn a person of danger
- o Physical evidence

I'll share a few stories with you, illustrating each of these types.

———————

Multiple Witnesses

If you are feeling skeptical, it is pretty easy to write off a simple encounter. Maybe the person was just misperceiving or imagining things, right? But what if more than one person reports experiencing the same thing? Are they both misperceiving in the same way? Both hallucinating the same thing?

Here is one example.

A man named Lee had a dog, Trixie. Trixie passed away. A week later, Lee's family was at breakfast. They heard Trixie barking in the dining room. They also heard her toenails clicking on the linoleum, as if she was running to the front door. Lee's mother absent-mindedly said, "Go see who it is at the door so early." Lee reminded her Trixie was dead; there was no dog to bark at someone at the front door. The mother said, "Oh, dear Lord."

Later, a neighbor dropped by and said, "I'm glad you got a new dog." The family was puzzled. They told the neighbor that they didn't have a new dog. But the neighbor insisted that she heard a dog barking at her when she was knocking at the door, earlier.[4]

We have Lee, his mother, other unspecified family members, and a neighbor all reporting auditory experiences of a "deceased" animal.

I found other accounts such as this, involving multiple witnesses. Most of them were auditory, with a couple being tactile in nature. If you would like to read more, please check the sources.[5]

Didn't Know They Were Dead

Skeptics typically dismiss ADCs as a trick of the brain – a hallucination subconsciously concocted to reduce grief. However, there are cases that tend to render that explanation impotent. I call them "DKD" cases for short – cases in which the person does not realize the animal is dead.

If ADCs are grief-induced hallucinations, then why do some people experience them when they do not know the animal is dead? Why would you need to hallucinate in order to relieve grief, if you don't know the animal is deceased? You wouldn't be experiencing grief over their death, because you don't know they are dead.

Here is an example. A woman named Susan Baker was watching a movie on TV, late at night. At one point, she instinctively reached down to pet her German Shepherd, Boo, who usually sat next to her on the floor. She felt her fingers running through the hair on Boo's neck. "Then I realized," Susan said, "that Boo was at the vet's." She said Boo had been in a lot of pain lately, so had taken her in for examination.

The ADC began as a tactile sensation, but then it turned visual. "I looked down," she said, "and there was Boo, looking at me with her soft and loving eyes." The next day, the vet called to tell her Boo had died that night.[4]

Her dog had been in pain, and she had taken her to the vet, so we can assume Susan was concerned about Boo. However, why would she have experienced a tactile and visual ADC of Boo, on the night she passed, without knowing that she had died? Why would she feel Boo, and see her appear, without Boo being present in the room? This is not a grief-induced hallucination, because there is no grief. As far as she knew, Boo was alive. If you think your dog is alive, you don't need to be reassured that your dog is alive "on the other side." Why is she feeling and seeing a "deceased" animal, when she does not know the animal is deceased? And what about the timing of the appearance, at the same time that Boo passes?

For other DKD cases, please check the sources.[5]

You will make up your own mind, of course, but after reading many of these DKD accounts, I am persuaded that they provide evidence that these people are not merely hallucinating; they are perceiving something real – an afterlife dimension of some sort.

―――――――

No Emotional Attachment

This is another type of case that refutes the common skeptical dismissal of these experiences. If ADCs are merely fantasies designed to alleviate grief over the loss of an animal, why would someone with no emotional attachment to the animal – who has no grief to alleviate – have an ADC of that animal?

S.P. Hipwell, a lecturer in Worcestershire, England, reported the following. He had a Doberman named Sophie. He said Sophie had a 260 word vocabulary. She died at the age of seven.

When alive, Sophie was very possessive of Mr. Hipwell's wife. She would not let anyone other than the immediate family sit next to her. "She would always force her bottom between them," he said.

He continued:

> "Even now, if someone sits by my wife on the settee,
> they can feel a pressure on their leg on the same
> side as my wife is sitting. Now this includes people

who are unaware of Sophie's existence. It occurred so regularly that we had to make a conscious effort to avoid the situation and the subsequent explanation."[6]

There are multiple witnesses to the tactile ADC – felt pressure on their leg, at the same side his wife is sitting, which is a behavior that corresponds to the dog's behavior when alive. And this includes people who did not know Sophie, therefore had no emotional attachment to her. This cannot be a grief-induced hallucination, because they had no grief. There is no indication that any of the witnesses are experiencing intense grief, but certainly the strangers to Sophie cannot be.

Other examples of tactile or auditory ADCs in the absence of emotional connection can be found in the sources.[5]

─────────

Rescue ADCs

"Rescue" ADCs occur with strange timing: they seem to warn a person of imminent danger and allow them to escape it. These reports are fairly uncommon – I counted only three, all of them auditory ADCs – but they are striking.

Here is one account, relayed by Bill Schul in his book, *Animal Immortality*.

Raymond Peters and his wife Suzanne had gone to bed after a long day. Their dog, Mac, had died three months ago.

About four hours after falling asleep, they were both awakened by a dog barking. Raymond recalls that, still half-asleep, he called out to his Scottie, Mac, to hush, and he remembers his wife saying, "What in the world is the matter with him?"

But Mac was not to be ignored. Raymond explained that there wasn't any way they could fall back asleep, for the next instant, Mac was frantically barking almost in his ear. Raymond sat up saying, 'Damn it, Mac,' thinking the dog wanted to go outside to urinate. But then he smelled smoke. Instantly wide awake, he leaped out of bed. Their bedroom door was closed, and when they opened it, choking smoke had already filled the hallway. They could feel the heat of the fire.

Raymond and Suzanne managed to rescue their children and escape the burning house. Minutes later, the house was engulfed in flames.

Bill Schul continued:

> *The fire department had been called by a neighbor who had been awakened by the barking dog. The sound had been so close, he said, that he first thought the dog was inside his own home. He then looked out the window for the dog and saw the flames.*
>
> *Only when the neighbor said to them, "My God, you would never have made it, if it hadn't been for your dog. I didn't know that you had gotten another dog after Mac died. Where is he, Ray? Did he get out of the house?"*
>
> *The Peters looked at each other, speechless for several moments. Raymond is not sure what he said at this point, but he recalls that it felt as though his heart had stopped, and he was dizzy. He heard Suzanne say, "Raymond... oh Raymond," as though frightened, and then himself saying, "It was Mac. I know Mac's bark. We've never had any other dog." No need to look for the Scottie, for he had made his exit three months previously.[6]*

If that is a hallucination, it sure is a fortunately well-timed one! But that is not a hallucination. First of all, the couple are not in grief. Mac died three months ago. Second, there are multiple witnesses – Raymond and Suzanne both hear Mac's bark; so does the neighbor, apparently. Nor is it plausibly a case of mistaken identity. Dog owners know the characteristic sound of their dogs' bark; they are as individual as human voices. Both Raymond and his wife recognized it as Mac's bark.

I believe that most ADCs have a purpose, but the purpose in rescue ADCs stands out in sharp relief, because of the timing. The ADC seems intended to warn the couple of imminent danger, and to allow them to escape it. It appears to be a conscious, deliberate act. It is hard to avoid seeing the ADC as a message, sent at specific time, for a specific purpose – not a hallucination, not wishful thinking, but a deliberate message, sent with a purpose.

———————

Physical Changes

In a couple of instances, there was something physical that supported the ADC report – perhaps physical movement that corresponded to the ADC, or, in the following case, a bit of physical evidence that seemed to corroborate it.

Alice Morgan had a brother, Phil, who died at age 8 of leukemia. The family had bought Phil a kitten to comfort him. The cat's name was Skitty, which is short for "Phil's kitty." Skitty died 8 years to the day after Phil died, and of a similar disease.

A year after Skitty died, Alice got married and moved into a new house. The previous owner had no cats, and Alice and her new husband did not have cats, because he was allergic to them.

Alice reported as follows:

> *"One evening the following summer, I awoke in the middle of the night to the sound of a cat leaping onto my bed. There is an odd, half-muffed 'mrrr' that cats say as they land after leaping; it is an unmistakable sound. I was startled but didn't want to wake my husband. I reached out in the darkness and felt a long-haired cat, about the size and fluffiness of Skitty. I felt for the ears. One had a V-shaped notch, just as Skitty had. It was incredible. [....]*
>
> *"The next morning as I was making the bed, I found several orange-buff cat hairs on my pillow, exactly the color of Skitty's fur. I looked at the calendar. The date was July 11, 1975."* Both Phil and Skitty had died on July 11th.[7]

In this case, we have a bit of physical data (the orange cat hairs on her pillow) that help to corroborate the ADC. Grief can be ruled out, since Skitty had been dead over a year at that point. The timing is remarkable for two reasons: first, because she found the cat hairs on the pillow right after having the ADC, and second, because the ADC occurred on the day of Phil and Skitty's death. There were no other cats in the house, so it wasn't another cat's hair. Unless you assume that Alice is lying, or that she hasn't washed her pillow case in over a year, then it is difficult to explain the account away in standard skeptical terms.

Auditory/Tactile/Olfactory ADC Wrap Up

Roughly half of the 103 auditory, tactile, and olfactory ADCs I reviewed were simple encounters, where you either take the person's word for it or you don't. The other half had additional corroborative factors – multiple witnesses, DKD, no emotional attachment, etc.

I related a few examples of the 103 accounts. Please read the sources cited below, if you would like to read more.[5] I've read hundreds of ADC accounts, and taken as a whole, I think they provide persuasive evidence of animal afterlife.

ADCs are the most common personal experience in this area. Most people will not experience an NDE, visit a medium, or have an OBE. But many of you – perhaps as many as 1 in 5 – will have an ADC of some sort. I have had my own experiences.

To be convinced by evidence and arguments is one thing, but personal experience is another. Although I rely on evidence and arguments in this book (in part because I realize that *my* personal experience is not going to mean much to *you*), once you have your own personal experience, things change. Even if others shrug their shoulders, your own personal experience can be very persuasive to you. Personal experience speaks in a way that arguments and external evidence cannot. And ADCs are the most common vehicle for personal experience.

ADCs are the most accessible route to knowing, at the level of personal experience, that animals have an afterlife. I hope that, when the time is right, you have your own. If not, don't sweat it; trying to make it happen will just interfere anyhow. You can always learn from the evidence and others' experiences.

Chapter 7

Mediumship

If you are familiar with the literature on mediumship, that will put you in a better position to appreciate the information that follows. Most people are not familiar with this literature. They see some mediums on TV, and they think maybe it's true, maybe it's fraud, and they don't think much more about it.

Here is a brief overview, for those of you who are new to the area. Literature on mediumship extends back at least 200 years. This literature includes thousands of detailed and impressive case reports, as well as careful, scientific investigations by reputable scientists. The overall literature provides good support for belief in an afterlife of some sort.

The history of mediumship is plagued with frauds and opportunists, though, so you have to be careful. Back in the heyday of mediumship, many people cashed in on the craze. Many frauds were caught and exposed. In modern times, the fraud continues. Some so-called "mediums" prey on the vulnerable. They often use what is called "cold-reading" techniques, which I'll discuss later.

However, the fact that fraudulent mediums exist does not mean that all mediums are fraudulent – any more than the fact that unethical therapists exist means that all therapists are unethical; or the fact that incompetent physicians exists means that all physicians are incompetent. There are unscrupulous people in every profession. That doesn't mean everyone in that profession is a liar and a crook. This is the white crow principle: just because you see a bunch of black crows doesn't mean all crows are black.

To be sure, mediumship is an unregulated profession, so frauds will be more prevalent there than in a regulated one. If you decide to consult a medium, be an educated consumer. I don't mean cynical; I mean educated. Do your homework.

Based on my reading, I believe the percentage of outright frauds is maybe 10 to 15%. The rest are people with a wide range of natural abilities and skill development. At the low end, there are those with very little genuine skill who may get an occasional "hit" but get by mostly with feel-good, non-specific statements and good interpersonal skills. At the other end are the gifted evidential mediums who are able to produce specific details they could not have known through normal means, which are then confirmed as valid. For example, they might say, "Your grandfather is here. His name begins with an H. Harry or Harold or something like that. He hears you when you talk to his picture on the mantle." The message contains specific details that the medium could not know through normal means. It is distinguished from a general statement such as, "I have your grandfather here. He loves you very much." While that may be true, it would also be easy to guess. Even the best mediums are not perfect; they achieve about an 85 or 90% hit rate.

If you are interested in learning more about the history of mediumship, and the literature it provides supporting survival beyond death, I have listed some sources in the notes.[1] In my view, the mediumistic literature provides good warrant for belief in an afterlife. It also provides some fascinating glimpses into that existence. It takes some serious study to understand it, so I would not suggest you bother with it if you do not have a serious, genuine interest. If you do become acquainted with the general literature, though, it will help you appreciate what mediums say about animal afterlife.

What About Animals?

As usual, the mediumship literature is focused almost exclusively on people. We are certainly our own favorite subject. And that literature provide persuasive evidence that human beings are cavorting around the afterlife. Good news for us humans, right?

But what about animals? Do mediums tell us that animals are part of the afterlife, too? Yes, they do. In fact, they do so nearly unanimously. I have heard many dozens of mediums speak on this subject – close to a hundred – and all of them, without exception, say that animals appear in their readings. When they tap into the "other side," animals are there. Whenever they are asked, "Are there animals in the afterlife?" their answer is always yes. I have never heard one say otherwise. I have never heard a medium deny it or say, "No, I never have had an animal come through in my readings." There may be an exception. There are thousands of mediums in the world; I have not listened to all of them. But I have never heard one deny that animals are in the afterlife. All of them say animals are there.

Kim Sheridan interviewed dozens of mediums about the subject. She said that the mediums "always stated that of course there were animals in the afterlife."[2] I have heard that same "of course" sentiment from mediums many times. They seem to be saying, "Why would it be otherwise?"

Mediumship reports of animals in the afterlife go back centuries. In the mid- to late-1800s, for instance, Hugh Benson and AD Mattson, two prominent mediums of the era, reported animals in their readings. And since then, animal afterlife has been universally attested to by mediums.

The consistency of the testimony is impressive. All of them say that animals are part of the afterlife. Are all of them wrong? Are all of them mistaken? If you understand the credibility, the character, and the track record of some of these mediums, it is difficult to justify that conclusion.

Even if you adopt a very cynical perspective and say the field is 90% frauds and cold readers, we don't need *all* of them to be right; we just need *one* of them to be. For the sake of argument, we only need one white crow.

Next, we will review six evidential mediumship cases.

Evidential Cases

I found 91 evidential cases in the literature. As I mentioned earlier, by "evidential," I mean that the medium is supplying detailed and specific information that he/she could not have obtained through normal means (through lucky guesses or "cold reading" techniques, for instance). If normal explanations can be ruled out, then it is more likely that the information is coming from exactly where the mediums say it is coming – another dimension that, for lack of a better word, we are calling the afterlife.

Here are six examples.

Rex

Slyvia Barbanell reported many evidential cases in her book, *When Your Animal Dies*. The animals coming through in readings included not just dogs and cats, but a one-eyed monkey, a donkey, a parrot, a cow, and two frogs named Adam and Eve.

Here is one of the cases Barbanell described.

A medium told a woman that she saw the spirit of a blue-eyed, bearded man whose name was William. He gave the time of his passing. He brought with him a dog with a bandaged paw. She could not catch the dog's full name but said it began with the letter 'R'.

The woman confirmed that William was her father's name, and the medium had correctly described his appearance and date of death. The dog was Rex, and while Rex was alive on Earth, his paw was frequently bandaged because he suffered from blisters between his toes.[3]

Notice the details – bandaged paw, name beginning with R, and information about her father. All of these details are confirmed by the sitter (the "sitter" is the person getting the reading).

———————

Rags

Here is another case from Sylvia Barbanell. It involves the DKD phenomenon – the sitter does not realize the animal is dead at the time of the reading.

Stella Hughes, a well-established evidential medium in England, was giving readings in a group. At one point, Stella turned to a woman in the group, described a dog, and then gave its name – Rags. The woman affirmed that the description matched her dog, and her dog was named Rags.

Stella then said to the woman that Rags had had been run over by a butcher's van. The woman shook her head and said no, she had no knowledge of that happening. However, when the woman returned home later, she learned that, in her absence, Rags had indeed been run over by a butcher's van.[3]

That case is noteworthy on several counts. First, Stella provides evidential material – she knows the woman owns a dog, describes the dog accurately; and gets the dog's name right. If you watch a lot of mediums, you'll notice how often they struggle with names, so getting the name right is no mean feat. And Rags is an unusual name.

Moreover, Stella knows – before the woman does – that the dog has died recently. She also knows specifically *how* the dog died – it was run over by a butcher's van (very specific). The woman denies it at the time, but she later confirms that both of these details were true: Rags is dead, run over by a butcher's van.

To assume that Stella is making lucky guesses is completely implausible. In addition, we see no evidence of cold reading techniques.

———————

Cold Reading

I need to pause for a moment to explain what I mean by cold reading. "Cold reading" describes a set of techniques used by unscrupulous mediums to fool gullible sitters into thinking they are getting "messages from beyond," when really they are getting manipulated and duped.

For example, one cold reading technique is to make plausible guesses and keep your statements general. "I'm getting a male who has passed. He is a father figure, or maybe an uncle. I'm feeling some strain in the relationship." The medium has observed the woman's age and deduced that her father is most likely deceased (I'm assuming she's a woman, because most people who get medium readings are women). Use of the word "figure" gives the medium additional wiggle room, in case her father and uncle are both alive. There is "some strain" in many relationships, so that is not a stretch. Chances are, the woman has had some relationship with a man that fits this description.

The medium using cold reading also pays close attention to non-verbal body language, then uses that to shape feedback. For instance, the medium might see signs of distress and pain in a person's eyes, when the subject of a deceased mother comes up. The medium may use that data and say, "Your mother says that she knows she hurt you. She is asking your forgiveness."

Another cold reading technique is to use questions to gather information, then later feed that information back to the sitter as if it is being "revealed." This sounds like an obvious ploy, but a skilled con artist can pull it off without detection.

Basically, the medium is using a bag of tricks to deceive the sitter. Telltale signs of cold reading include leading questions, vague statements, or statements that could be easily guessed. In my experience, these mediums also play up the theatrics; they exude showmanship in a way that sets off my alarm bells.

———————

Doubting Tres

Returning to the examples now. Kim Sheridan relayed this case.

A woman named Tres had a dog who passed away. Tres described herself as "having always been a 'Doubting Thomas' about near-death experiences, the afterlife, etc." However, she experienced signs of her dog's presence after his death, and that opened her mind. She decided to attend a public mediumship reading.

Tres reported:

> "I spoke to no one and knew no one there, so there was no way anyone knew anything about me. I was the third person chosen by the medium, and she said a few things that were correct [....]

> "Then she said, "I want you to know that dogs and other animals go to the other side. I tell you this because you love dogs and there is a very large one standing behind you with her paws on your shoulders right now. You have been talking to her picture every day and weeping. She said she had her own chair in your house and not to cry; she is with you.

> "Well, that was it. I broke down and sobbed uncontrollably." [4]

The medium provides specific details that she could not have known through normal means – that Tres had a dog; that the dog is very large; that Tres is there because her dog died, and that Tres has been talking to her picture and crying every day. It's also significant that Tres was a stranger to the group, spoke to no one, and described herself as a skeptic.

––––––––––

Roast Beef and Brio

Elena Mannes, who won 18 awards for journalism, described herself as hard-nosed and skeptical person by nature, a materialist/atheist for most of her life. The death of her dog, Brio, though, catalyzed a process that took her from atheist to believer. In her book, *Soul Dog*, Elena relates that story. Many interesting moments occur around evidential medium readings of Brio.

Here, Elena is speaking with a medium named Dawn, following the death of Brio.

> *"I told Dawn nothing of the last days with Brio, nothing of my experience during those last moments of his passing. "I sat under a little tree and ate roast beef" were the first words out of Dawn's mouth. "He enjoyed the moment," she went on. "He wants you to feel him there in that*

spot." I'd said nothing about how I had in fact sat with Brio in the yard and fed him an entire pound of roast beef." [5]

Dawn somehow knows that Elena sat under a tree and fed Brio roast beef before he died. That is a pretty specific detail. You can't just guess something like that or use cold reading techniques to get it.

Elena visited several other animal mediums. All of them provided specific, accurate information that they could not have obtained through normal means. Furthermore, the accounts reinforced and corroborated each other.

Despite lifelong atheism and a belief that there was nothing outside this physical existence, Elena became convinced through these mediumship readings and other experiences that her dog had survived. She was convinced enough to admit that her worldview had been wrong, and to write a book about it, exposing herself to the risk of embarrassment and damage to her reputation.

Jumbo the Dog

Harold Sharp related this account. A friend of his, Sarah Chester, has died. Sarah had a dog, Jumbo, who died before Sarah.

Harold wrote:

> *Sometime afterwards, I had a sitting with Mrs. Neville [a medium], who said, "There is a woman here, and she is about 60 years of age. She is saying 'Chester' – that is probably her name or the name of the town where she lived. She has a big shaggy dog with her, she calls him Jumbo. And she is dressed in tweeds and is just off for a walk with her dog. My word, they are an energetic pair."*

Mrs. Neville picks up the woman's name, her approximate age and manner of dress, the dog's name, and a specific description of the dog. Those are very specific details that could not be guessed or derived through cold reading.

Choo Choo

One more case, this one from Karen Anderson, a well-regarded animal medium with a background in law enforcement. Karen is reading for a woman whose cat, Choo Choo, has recently passed away.

> *Karen: "Choo Choo is showing me her whiskers and keeps brushing them against my face, and it tickles. Choo Choo*

says this is how she wakes you up. Do you understand this message?"

Woman: "Oh my gosh! Do I understand it? Yes, I do! Choo Choo would wake me up every morning with her whiskers. I miss her so much. Does she know how much I love her?" their mom asked, choking back the tears.

Karen: "Yes, she does. She says you talk to her all the time and that she still wakes you up with her whiskers," Karen said.

Woman: "I thought I was going crazy, but I can still feel her whiskers brush against my face. Is that really her?" their mom asked, barely able to talk.

Karen: "Yes, that's her. She says she helps you wake up on time."

Woman: "Unbelievable. I just can't wrap my head around how this is possible."

Karen: "Now Choo Choo is showing me a plate of sushi. Does that make any sense to you?"

Woman: "Yes! Sushi was her name when I adopted her from the shelter. It didn't suit her, so I changed it to Choo Choo. Nobody knows that, Karen. How did you know?"

Karen: "Choo Choo told me."

Karen is giving detailed, specific information – whiskers brushing up against the woman's face, the timing of the behavior, the purpose of the behavior, the fact that the woman is still experiencing it, and the cat's name prior to adoption, which no one except the woman knew.

The probability of Karen guessing all of those details correctly is infinitesimally small. If you like playing with numbers and would like to estimate the combined probability of her guessing all of that by chance, just estimate the individual probability of guessing each detail, then multiply those probabilities together. When I did that, I came up with a combined probability of 1 in 16 million of getting all that correct just by chance. Even if you think my estimate is way off, I suspect you would agree that the odds of her guessing all of those details are ridiculously low.

There is no indication of cold reading. Cold readers use a lot of "fishing" questions, which Karen doesn't, and they give broad, general statements (e.g., "Your cat loves you"), not specific details they have no way of knowing.

That gives you a sample of evidential mediumship on this topic. I believe these cases defy explanation through ordinary means (fraud, lucky guesses, cold reading). Common skeptical explanations just don't hold up in these instances. And there are many others like them.

Animal Greeters

While we are on the subject of mediumship, I have to pass on this little nugget from Dr. Julia Assante. Dr. Assante is a scholar of the ancient Near East, and she is also a medium. Dr. Assante stated that, although the most common "greeters" in the afterlife are grandparents, the second-most common, in her experience, are animals:

> I think 10 percent of all spontaneous afterlife encounters are with pets. That's huge. That's higher than a spouse, higher than a sibling. I have seen a lot of people go over, and those who greet them first are their old pets. Often our pets will hang out with other family members, whether or not they ever knew them while they were in the body.[9]

Telepathy

There is one plausible alternative explanation that we should discuss: telepathy. Maybe the medium is just reading the mind of the sitter, rather than communicating with an animal on the other side? That might be possible. After all, the sitter knows most of the information the medium is presenting. There is good evidence that telepathy can occur.[8] If the medium can read the sitter's mind, maybe that is where she is getting the information, not from a soul in the afterlife?

I can't do this subject justice without going off on a very long tangent, which I will spare you. I will say a few words, though, then refer to you to some other sources for more discussion.

Telepathy cannot be definitively ruled out as a potential explanation in many of these cases. However, it is a poor explanation for many other cases, and it does not seem to be an adequate explanation for evidential mediumship as a whole.

There are many cases in which the information obtained by the medium is *not present* in the mind of the sitter. The medium receives accurate and detailed information that is not known to the sitter at the time. It is only later verified to be true. Because the sitter is unaware of the information, telepathy cannot explain the results. The medium can't be getting the information by reading the sitter's mind, because the information is not *in* the sitter's mind.

There are many cases like this in the general mediumship literature. Most DKD cases would fall into this category. There are some cases like this in the animal literature as well. We saw one earlier – the case of Rags, run over by a butcher's van. The medium knew the information, but the dog's owner did not. Telepathy cannot explain that. There are many other DKD cases.

Secondly, according to the work of Dr. Julie Beischel, who has studied mediums for decades, mediums are able to tell the difference between telepathy and mediumship. They can tell the difference between information coming from a live person as opposed to a "dead" one. Mediums describe this as operating in two different modes, each with a different feel and process.

Mediumship and telepathy appear to be different skill sets as well. Dr. Beischel's research supports that distinction. She has found both qualitative and quantitative differences in these two modes, including differences in neuroimaging. [10]

The explanation via telepathy, then, disregards what experienced mediums tell us about their own experience. Are they not the experts on their own skills and experience? Mediums say that telepathy and mediumship are different skill sets and processes, and that the phenomenological differences are palpable. Those differences appear on neuroimaging. Are we to disregard all that?

Granted, we cannot definitively rule out telepathy as a possible explanation for some cases. However, it has a number of weaknesses as a general explanation. It cannot account for many cases. It runs contrary to what experienced evidential mediums tell us about their own processes. It is not an adequate explanation for mediumship in general.

Some proponents of the telepathy explanation have expanded the notion to something they call SuperPsi, which is able to leap tall objections in a single bound. I'll leave it there, though. If you'd like read more about this, please check the suggestions below. [11]

A Controlled Experiment

I was surprised to stumble across a controlled, scientific experiment on mediumship and animal afterlife. As I mentioned in the Introduction, controlled, scientific experiments in the area of human afterlife studies are very rare. Forget about animals. So I was stunned to find it. Granted, it's just a single study, and we should never make too much out of a single study, but still, it's something, and worth a look.

Dr. Julie Beischel at her colleagues at Windbridge Institute have been investigating and testing mediums for decades. They use quadruple-blinded protocols, which is a level of control that far exceeds that used in most experiments.

"Blinding" refers to experimental controls that ensure that the experimenter and participants don't inadvertently, subconsciously affect the outcome of the study. In Dr. Beischel's protocols, it means that the medium, the proxy sitter (a neutral person sitting in for the actual target of the reading), the real person for whom the reading is intended, and any intermediaries handling the data are all blinded to (unaware of) who is who and which is which.

Dr. Beischel has imposed these high levels of control in order to deal with escalating skeptical objections. When earlier research showed significant results, skeptics argued that the information was slipping somehow – leaked by the person getting the reading, leaked by the proxy sitter, or somehow distorted by the experimenters themselves. Despite the artificiality of quadruple blinded conditions (not how mediums normally operate in the real world), significant results are still obtained, demonstrating that some mediums are able to pick up specific, detailed information that they do not have access to through normal means. [12]

Here is the abstract summary for Dr. Beischel's study on mediumship involving animals:

Using a full-blinded protocol similar to that employed to test mediumship accuracy during readings for deceased people, exploratory and ongoing research has demonstrated that some mediums can report accurate and specific information about deceased companion animals as well. [13]

That is, some mediums in this research were able to get accurate, specific details about "deceased" pets. They did so despite the fact that they were operating under many artificial constraints.

Where are the mediums getting their information? Alternative explanations (including fraud, cold reading, guessing, and even telepathy) are ruled out by the experimental controls. Dr. Beischel is appropriately cautious about the implications of her research, but she says that the most reasonable explanation for the results is that mediums are getting the information from exactly where they saying they are getting it – from "discarnate" individuals (in this case, animals) on the other side.

Mediumship Wrap Up

The mediumship literature supports a belief in animal afterlife in several ways.

First, there is a general consensus among mediums. I have heard nearly a hundred mediums answer the question, "Do animals have an afterlife?" All of them have stated that animals are present in the afterlife. There may be exceptions, but I am not aware of them, and if exceptions do exist, they are a small minority, vastly outnumbered. The overwhelming consensus among mediums is that animals exist in the afterlife.

Second, we sampled half a dozen of the 91 evidential cases I found in the literature. No doubt there are more scattered about the internet, not included here. These mediums are conveying specific and detailed information about "deceased" animals that they could not obtain through normal means (fraud, guessing, cold reading, etc.).

Third, we have one well-controlled experiment conducted by an experienced scientist, suggesting that some mediums can obtain evidential data about "deceased" animals, despite high levels of experimental control.

As I mentioned before, whether you find this information credible will depend in part on your familiarity with general mediumship literature. Once you see the pattern in the general literature, it is easier to see here.

You will make up your own mind, of course, but in my view, the mediumship literature provides a strong pillar of support for belief in animal afterlife.

Chapter 8

Physical Mediumship

I wanted to split this chapter off from the one on mediumship, because what is called "physical mediumship" differs dramatically from "normal" (mental) mediumship. It is a different animal entirely, and it boggles the mind in a way that "normal" mediumship may not – and, for most modern people, normal mediumship is already difficult enough to swallow. When you add the weirdness inherent in physical mediumship – tables tipping, voices manifesting out of thin air, objects materializing in a darkened room – then it becomes a bridge too far for most people. I get that. There are reasons to be skeptical. The sessions take place in the dark, which immediately raises suspicion of trickery. And physical mediumship has been plagued by a history of fraud.

I should stop to clarify what I mean by "physical mediumship," for those unfamiliar with it. In "normal" (or mental) mediumship, the mediumistic exchange of information happens in the mind. The medium receives thoughts, feelings, and images from the "deceased" individual. In physical mediumship, though, the transmission takes physical form. In the earliest examples, there were rapping noises, tables tipping or lifting off the ground, and objects moving. Later, there was automatic/involuntary writing, voices speaking through a materialized "trumpet" in the air, or objects materializing. In the more dramatic cases, "deceased" individuals make an appearance in semi-physical form (e.g., face, hands).

Mental (or what I'm calling "normal") mediumship is much more common than physical. Proficient physical mediums are rare. Frauds were abundant, especially back in the mid-1800s, when everyone was trying to cash in on the craze. The fact that it happens in a dark room makes it easier to fake.

There are some well-documented, impressive cases of physical mediumship, though. Some of these mediums have been tested under very strict conditions – the room checked carefully beforehand, the medium strapped tightly to a chair, with hands and feet bound, mouth taped shut. Leslie Flint was one such medium; a large collection of his recordings is available through the Leslie Flint Trust.[1]

In her book, Surviving Death, journalist Leslie Kean describes her investigation of physical mediums Kai Muegge and Stewart Alexander. She has some impressive experiences of her own along the way. If you wonder about whether there is anything legitimate going on with physical mediumship, her book is well worth a read.[2]

Despite my initial skepticism, I have been persuaded by my reading and viewing that at least some instances of physical mediumship are bona fide. If you would like to read some overviews of the topic, I have listed some sources in the notes.[3]

Animals in Physical Mediumship

I found 25 reports of animals in physical mediumship. In some cases, the animals were described by "deceased" humans, and in other cases, the animals manifested physically. Animals included dogs, cats, birds, horses, squirrels, ferrets, and monkeys.

Twenty five reports underestimates the actual number. In his book, *Life After Death*, Neville Randall summarizes the recordings of Leslie Flint, who I mentioned earlier. Flint was a direct voice medium – someone who produced the recognizable voices of deceased individuals, not through his own vocal cords, but from a source outside him.

Flint was subject to high levels of scrutiny. He was able to produce remarkable results even when his arms and legs were being held, his mouth taped shut and filled with liquid, and the proceedings inspected by experienced scientists and debunkers.

In many cases, the "deceased" people who were speaking through Leslie attested to the presence of animals in the afterlife. In his book, Randall gives three examples of this, but he indicates that these are only a small sample, and that "many more" accounts of animals exist in Leslie Flint's recordings.

Over 2000 recordings are archived at leslieflint.com. I could not search the archive for individual animal appearances, so I can only guess how many feature animals. If we use the percentages from the NDE and ADC studies (15% and 16%, respectively), we can estimate that about 300 of those recordings feature animals. I admit that is just a guess, but I think it's safe to say the number is in the hundreds.

Here is one example, shared by Randall.

Old Jenny

George Wilmot owned a horse named Old Jenny. In one session, George's voice came through Leslie Flint. George said that, after he died and passed over, he was astonished to be greeted by his old horse, Jenny. Jenny used to pull George's merchant cart, when George was in his 30's.

George (through Leslie Flint) said:

"I was real upset when poor old Jenny collapsed and died. She was as near to me as any woman could be, in fact more so. [George mentions that he had parted ways with two wives, who were "no bloody good."] I had great affection for old Jenny. She knew everything that I ever said to her; I'm sure she did.... She wasn't much to look at, I suppose, as horses go, but she was a real nice old nag.

"The first thing I remember when I [died and] woke up over here [in the afterlife] was being in a – well, I suppose you'd call it a field. I seemed to be sitting, lying, under a tree. I remember waking up. I could

see this horse coming towards me, and there was my old Jenny!

'She looked younger, of course, and she was so thrilled and so happy, you could sense and feel it. I can't say how. This is something I can't explain. But it was almost as if she was talking to me. It was extraordinary. I couldn't hear any voice, and you don't expect to hear a horse speak, but it was somehow mentally [transmitted], I suppose."

"It was as if she was speaking to me and welcoming me. She came beside me and was licking my face. Goodness me, I'll never forget this as long as I live, I was so thrilled and excited and patting and fussing her." 4

Shock the Monkey

Here is another example. It comes from Harold Sharp, who owned a pet Monkey named Mickey, who was deceased at the time of this story.

Harold said that when Mickey was alive, he had a tendency to pick through his fur in search of bits of crystalized salt. Harold explained that this salt was a "tasty morsel" for monkeys. Harold said that when most people see monkeys doing this, they don't understand the purpose, and they misinterpret it as picking at fleas.

Harold described his pet monkey, Mickey, as "vain," and said he was sensitive on this subject. He said, "If anyone accused Mickey of flea-hunting, he felt it a great indignity and became angry."

Years after Mickey passed away, Harold was sitting in a physical mediumship circle. "I suddenly became aware of a considerable weight on my knee," he said. The medium turned to Harold and said, "Do not move, Mr. Sharp. There is a lovely large monkey materializing on your knee." Mickey gradually became visible.

Then Mickey started picking at his fur, in his characteristic way. The medium saw this, and he chided him: "No, no, Mickey, you must not catch fleas in public!" He made the common misinterpretation of the behavior. And at that point, Mickey disappeared. Harold says he was offended. [5]

I find this account humorous. You probably find it hard to believe – materializing monkeys? – but it has some elements worth considering. First, the medium did not know of Mickey or his death. He knew nothing of Mr. Sharp's love of monkeys or about Mickey in particular. Second, there were multiple witnesses. Third, Mickey's disappearance corresponded with the medium's chiding him about an apparently touchy subject.

Harold Sharp recounts several more stories like this in his book, *Animals in the Spirit World*.

Full Dog

One more example, this one from Slyvia Barbanell. It involves a dog, fully materialized.

Slyvia reports:

> *A well-known medium, Mr. Charles Glover Botham, used to hold a materialization home circle where, on one occasion the sitters were very surprised when a materialized form of a large dog suddenly appeared. He bounded forward in a most energetic manner and proceeded to jump excitedly from one sitter to another, resting his paws on their knees and sometimes licking a hand or a face.*
>
> *The animal seemed thoroughly to enjoy the amount of affection and interest displayed by the members of the circle, most of whom were great animal lovers. The dog ran to a bowl of water that was always provided at the seances for psychic purposes [it is said to facilitate the energy]. The materialized animal proceeded to lap up the water eagerly and noisily, as though the excitement had made him thirsty. Afterwards, the bowl was found to be completely empty. There was not a drop of spilled water to be seen anywhere.* [7]

Reports of full materializations like this are rare. Admittedly, they are difficult for me to believe; at the same time, though, I find them difficult to just brush off as fraudulent. Most cases involve something more modest, like a bark or a partial appearance. See Sylvia Barbanell's book for other examples.

––––––––––

Those are a few of the 25 cases I found in the literature, where animals make an appearance in physical mediumship. That is a significant underestimate. At the Leslie Flint site alone, there are probably hundreds of other cases, and no doubt there are many more unpublished or scattered about the internet.

I understand if you are skeptical of these reports. Physical mediumship provokes incredulity in ways that NDEs or even mental mediumship do not. However, there is evidence that at least some of these phenomena are not just magic tricks or gullibility; some of it is "real," in some sense.[3] Also, it's worth noting that, since it takes place in a group, the phenomena has multiple witnesses.

Remember the white crow principle, too. We don't need all of these reports to be valid; we just need one of them to be. That is enough to demonstrate animal afterlife.

Chapter 9

The Blob:

Group Souls for Animals?

There is a common idea in the afterlife literature on animals, which I want to spend a bit of time dismantling. If you read this literature, as I do, you'll often come across the idea that, when animals die, they return to "group souls." The idea first popped up in channeled material in the 19th century. It resurfaces periodically. It gets passed around, sort of like received wisdom, usually without much examination.

The basic idea is that when animals die, they get re-absorbed back into a humungous group soul. Think of the group soul as being a generalized archetype for the species. When animals die, so the story goes, they do not continue on as individual spirits but instead are assimilated, Borg-like, back into a big amorphous blob that represents the species.

Individual pigs don't live on as individual pigs; they are absorbed back into the big amorphous Pig soul. Rabbits don't live on as individual rabbits; they are sucked back into Rabbit. Whatever individual features they might have had are wiped out. Only the common characteristics of the species remain.

147

Each species has its own group soul. Well, except for human beings – we're special. We have individual spirits and individualized afterlife experience. Animals don't – or so the story goes. They get reabsorbed back into the group soul.

Hearing this, you may worry that your dog or cat is bound for amorphous blobbery. However, there is a loophole. The loophole goes like this: if a human being cares for (loves) an animal, then that animal is granted an individualized spirit. That animal escapes being absorbed into the Big Blob at the end of his or her life. Instead, that animal lives on as an individual spirit. The human being's care and love confers individuality upon it.

Unfortunately, other animals are out of luck. If a human being does not confer love or care upon them, they are returned to the Big Blob at death. Whatever individuality they might have is gone.

I think that is nonsense. Specifically, I think these two ideas are wrong:

1. That when animals die, they return to a group soul, an amorphous blob in which individuality is erased.

2. An animal can be granted an individual soul (and escape amorphous blobbery) if a human being loves and cares for that animal. Animals who are not bonded to humans will be returned to the Blob.

Before talking about why those ideas are wrong, I need to clarify that I am talking about "group souls," not "soul groups." You'll see both terms used in afterlife literature, and they sound similar, so it's easy to get them mixed up. But they are different concepts.

A "soul group" is a set of people or other beings that are spiritually connected. NDErs, mediums, and other afterlife explorers have reported that, when you die, you rejoin your soul group. Soul groups are basically families of kindred spirits, based not necessarily on earthly ties but on level of development, shared values, or perspective. Individuality is fully preserved in a soul group. A soul group is by definition a family of individuals. I've got no beef with soul groups.

A "group soul," though, is a very different concept. That's what I'm talking about. A "group soul" is a single, unitary entity. It is an amorphous, generalized archetype for the species, into which all members are absorbed at death, like raindrops rejoining the sea. Individuality is not preserved in a group soul. Individuality only exists at the species level – a Dog group soul is different than a Cat group soul, for instance, but individual dogs and cats cease to exist as individuals, unless a human being confers individuality and separate existence upon them with their love.

That's the idea of group souls for animals. That is what I think is nonsense.

Let's get into it. I have six points to make.

You Might as Well Be Dead

If you are reabsorbed into a group soul, you might as well be dead. Assimilation into an amorphous, species-level blob is not an afterlife existence in any meaningful sense of the term.

To see this, just apply the idea of group souls to yourself. What if, when you died, everything that made you *you* – your personality, memories, and knowledge – was all wiped away, and you were reabsorbed into an anonymous, amorphous blob called Human Being? What sort of afterlife existence would you have?

Whatever sort of afterlife that would be, *you* would not be there to experience it.

To see this even more clearly, imagine the same idea applied to your loved ones. What if, when the people you loved died – parents, siblings, friends, children – everything that made them unique individuals was wiped out, and they were assimilated into a big blob called Human Being? Do they even exist anymore, in any meaningful sense? They have been reduced to a category.

If who you are disappears when you die, you might as well be dead. *You* are not there anymore to experience it.

This is a pretty easy concept to grasp, when we apply it to ourselves or our human loved ones. Sometimes, it can be harder see when it comes to animals – or rather, harder to see as a problem.

I think that's because people often don't think of animals as having individuality in the first place. One bear is the same as the next; one wolf the same as the next; one robin the same as the next, and so forth. Because they see animals as interchangeable units, they aren't bothered by the idea of animals being absorbed into an anonymous blob. They don't see them as individuals in the first place.

That is a mistaken view. I'll get to that in a minute, but for now, I just want to be clear what the idea of group souls implies. It implies that there is no afterlife for animals -- not in any meaningful sense of the term. At death, animals are swallowed up into an amorphous blob, reduced to a generalized category label. That animal's life is effectively over; they are done and dusted.

We recoil when that idea is applied to us, because we understand the implications. When applied to us, the idea of group souls means we cease to exist; we have no real afterlife. Maybe we should think twice before applying the same idea to animals.

_____

The Evidence Contradicts It

When we examine the evidence for animal afterlife, we discover something interesting: all the evidence contradicts the notion of group souls. All the evidence indicates that animals survive into the next world as individuals.

People who have After-Death Communications never see an archetypal Horse. They always see a particular, individual horse.

When a cat appears in an NDE, it's always a specific cat, never a generalized spirit of Cat. When someone sees a dog in a Deathbed Vision, it's always a particular dog, never a global, undifferentiated Dog. When evidential mediums bring through information from a deceased animal, it's always from a specific, individual animal, never from an archetypal representation of the species. When people see ghosts, they always describe a particular, identifiable animal, not an amorphous category.

This is important. All of the evidence we have about animal afterlife indicates that animals survive death as individuals. All of the evidence contradicts the idea of group souls.

What about the corollary loophole, though? Maybe you're thinking, "Yes, but these animals were loved by people. That's why they survived as individuals."

Two things about that. First, not all of these animals were cared for by human beings. For instance, some of the ghost sightings involve animals who were neglected or even tortured by human beings. We also have NDE and ADC reports of animals who have no discernable connection to any human being. There are many cases in which animals appear as individuals, yet there is no evidence of human caring at all. If this evidence is to be trusted, then it disproves the corollary loophole. Animals do not require human beings to give them individuality in the afterlife.

Second, the idea underpinning this loophole -- that human beings bestow individuality upon animals -- is a silly conceit. I'll cover that shortly.

For now, just notice that all the evidence runs counter to the idea of group souls. In all the evidence we have, animals always appear as individual spirits, never as generalized archetypes. I am not aware of any credible reports of animals communicating in the form of amorphous group souls. Animals only appear in individualized form. That is true across all the areas of evidence we have considered.

All the evidence, then, refutes the idea of group souls for animals. It indicates that animals live on as individuals. They do not get reduced to an amorphous blob. They retain their individuality after death, just like we do.

————

Human Hubris

I mentioned above that the corollary loophole, which says that if an animal is cared for by a human being, then that animal is granted individuality of soul and spared the fate of anonymous blobbery, is a silly conceit. Let me say a little more about that.

Just think about it. The idea is that the love of a human being, the relationship with a human being, is so powerful and magnificent that it is able bestow individuality upon lesser creatures and rescue them from anonymous blobbery.

I chuckle as I write that. We sure do think highly of ourselves. Where did this ridiculous idea come from? From our usual hubris, I'm guessing.

Do we really believe that being connected to a human being is enough to bestow individuality upon other species? Are we really that grandiose and self-centered? Do we really think that our mere care can confer individuality of soul? And that without our care, all animals are doomed to be assimilated into the Big Blob? Do we think we are some sort of spiritual King Midas, that everything we touch is turned to individuality? Please.

David Fontana says it well:

> It is sometimes suggested that if animals survive, they only retain their individuality in the afterlife if they have lived close to humans and been "given" individuality through human love. Otherwise, they return to the collective consciousness of their species. This claim typifies our rather self-centered way of thinking. As humans, we regard ourselves as lords of creation, with every other life form subservient to us, and open to our exploitation.
>
> But there is no special warrant for this view, and it would be arrogant to suppose that our assumed superiority will persist in the next world. It may be that one of the lessons we would have to learn in an afterlife is the unity of all existence, with all of creation arising from the same source. [2]

In addition to the grandiosity involved in this notion, we also have evidence against it. As I mentioned earlier, there are many afterlife cases involving animals who have no emotional connection with a human being, or who have received only hostility, abuse, and neglect. All of these cases refute the idea that human love is required to grant animals an individual afterlife.

―――――――――

Animals are Already Individuals

Animals already possess individuality. They don't need us to confer individual upon them. It is egotistical to think so.

Ask any biologist who studies animals. They will tell you that of course animals are individuals. All wolves are not all the same. All elephants are not the same. All parrots are not the same. Yes, they have traits in common with other members of their species – as we do – but they also have things that distinguish them from each other. Not just physical differences (size, gender, coloration, etc.), but mental, emotional, and behavioral differences. They show differences in terms of their personalities, temperaments, learning histories (i.e., emotional programming, understanding of the world), and behavioral tendencies.

In other words, they are individuals.

Thomas Merton has a beautiful passage where he talks about the individuality of everything God created. For those of you who don't like God language, ignore that part and just try to listen behind it, to what he's saying about the individuality of everything in nature.

> *This particular tree will give glory to God by spreading out its roots in the earth and raising its branches into the air and the light in a way that no other tree before or after it ever did or will do. The special clumsy beauty of this particular colt on this April day in this field under these clouds is a holiness consecrated to God by His own creative wisdom. The pale flowers of the dogwood outside this window are saints. The little yellow flowers nobody notices on the edge of that road are saints looking up into the face of God. This leaf has its own texture and its own pattern of veins and its own holy shape.... The great, gashed, half-naked mountain is another of God's saints. There is no other like him. He is alone in his own character; nothing else in the world ever did or ever will imitate God in quite the same way.* [1]

Naturalists, animal breeders, and monks know that animals are individuals. So does anyone who has spent significant time around animals. Animals don't need us to grant them individuality. They already have it. Animals already have different personalities, different behaviors, and different temperaments.

156

That is true for both domestic and wild animals. It is true for animals who have been loved by humans and for those who have not.

If animals possess individuality in life, why would they would lose that individuality in the afterlife? All the evidence points in the opposite direction.

———————

Anachronism

The idea of group souls for animals is based on statements made by some mediumistic channels in the 19th century (e.g., Allan Kardec). Although you still hear this notion being passed around occasionally, it is much less common than it was back then. In fact, most mediums today contradict it. They speak about animals having individual spirits and make no reference to group souls.

How do we account for this discrepancy? Why would mediums in the 19th century talk about group souls but modern mediums not?

I think it's because mediumship relies in part on the interpretive framework of the medium. Mediums are people, and they are affected by the cultural beliefs of the time. You can see this in many ways – e.g., in the highly religious imagery of some 19th century mediums, compared to the absence of that imagery in most of today's mediumship.

Mediums don't simply report what they receive, as if they are taking transcription. Messages come to them in images, feelings, thoughts, and fragments – which they try to translate and make sense of. In other words, the medium does not simply receive and relay a message directly; he or she is an intermediary and *interprets* the message.

That is how human communication works: there is a sender, and there is a receiver. Breakdowns in communication can happen at either end (sender, receiver) or in between. Part of the process requires the receiver to interpret the sender's message accurately. But this often does not happen. One reason why is that the receiver's interpretive framework is shaped by his/her own experiences, beliefs, and expectations.

This happens in mediumship. The medium must use their own framework to interpret the messages they receive. That framework is built from their belief systems, experiences, and expectations – which are inevitably shaped by the era in which the medium resides.

In the 19th century, animals were generally considered to be dumb brutes – unfeeling, barely sentient, largely indistinguishable from one another. Mediums operating in the 19th century would naturally be influenced by those cultural beliefs. In turn, that would affect their interpretations of the messages received.

I think that is how the notion of group souls for animals came to be – as a misinterpretation of the messages being received, distorted by cultural beliefs of the time. As our culture has learned more about animals, our beliefs about animals have changed. We see them as individuals in a way we did not, two centuries ago. As a result, we hear less about "group souls" and more about animals as individual spirits. As the culture has changed, so have the attitudes and beliefs of mediums. As a result, messages received by mediums are put in a different context.

The idea of "group souls" is an anachronism. It is a reflection of how people viewed animals in the 19th century – as dumb brutes indistinguishable from one another. We know better now, and we need to drop this outdated idea.

––––––––––

Crude Microscopes

I think of group souls as akin to how scientists thought about the cell, a hundred years ago. Back then, scientists had only a simple microscope. When they looked through it at the cell, they saw an amorphous blob. They thought the cell was a simple thing, filled with a goo they called protoplasm.

Fast forward a hundred years. Scientists developed the electron microscope. Now they can see more deeply and clearly into the cell.

What do they see now? Not an amorphous blob of undifferentiated protoplasm – not at all. They see the exact opposite: an incredibly complicated, interacting organization of thousands of differentiated parts, working together in a finely tuned symphony. A cell makes the most complex feats of high-tech engineering look like child's play.

A hundred years ago, scientists believed cells were simple, amorphous blobs. Today, because of better observational equipment, we know that the cell is a mind-bogglingly complex system of individualized and exquisitely coordinated, interacting parts.

I believe that something analogous is happening with the idea of group souls. Some people have looked through their crude microscopes and seen an amorphous blob, which they called a group soul.

When our observational tools get better, we will be able to see more clearly. The picture will change, just as it did for the scientists looking at the cell. What once looked like a featureless blob will resolve itself into something of enormous variety and complexity.

Fight the Blob

In my view, the idea of group souls for animals is just flat wrong. I'll reiterate the main reasons:

- o It means that there is no real afterlife for animals.

- o All of the evidence we have refutes it. All the evidence shows that animals survive in individualized form, not as global archetypes.

- o The idea that human love confers individuality upon animal spirits is nothing but a silly conceit.

- o As naturalists, animal behaviorists, monks, and anyone who's ever known an animal will tell you, animals are already individuals. They do not need us to confer individuality upon them.

- o The idea is a holdover from an earlier era, when society conceived of animals as dumb, insentient brutes.

We should disregard the notion that animals are returned to amorphous "group souls" after death. That idea is anachronistic and contradicted by the evidence. Animals are individuals, both here and in the hereafter. When their physical body dies, they continue on as individuals, just as we do.

Chapter 10

Deathbed Visions

A deathbed vision (DBV) occurs in the minutes, or hours, or days before death. The dying person may suddenly become alert, gaze at a spot where nothing appears to be, and express happiness. They may reach out their hands, as if to make contact with something or someone. And then they pass away shortly thereafter.

Reports of DBVs date back millennia. They have been reported in nearly every culture on Earth. Only about 10% of dying people are conscious as they approach death, research suggests that, of those who are conscious, about half of them have DBVs of some sort.[1]

Among those who report DBVs, 70% say they see a deceased loved one – a parent, grandparent, other relative, or friend. In the other 30% of cases, they see either a spiritual being or a beautiful natural landscape.

Hardcore materialist skeptics, of course, brush these off as hallucinations or brain dysfunction. From what I have read, DBV researchers have examined many of these skeptical counter-explanations for DBVs – hallucination, medical condition, medication, oxygen deprivation, pre-existing religious beliefs, etc.

– and found them all wanting. None of them hold up very well. As is the case in other areas (e.g., NDEs, mediumship), these explanations seem held to on the basis of faith in a materialistic worldview, rather than on any particular evidence. It is just *assumed* that they are hallucinations, because, on a materialistic worldview, what else could they be?

Here are a few things that suggest DBVs are more than mere hallucinations or brain dysfunctions.

First, there is the timing. People having a DBV will often say something to an apparently empty space in the room, such as "I'll be there in just a minute," and then die shortly thereafter. If they are hallucinating, why is it so well-timed?

Sometimes, a patient with severe dementia who has been comatose or incoherent for years suddenly wakes up, speaks with perfect clarity about a DBV encounter, then lapses into unconsciousness and dies. This is known as terminal lucidity – sudden, remarkable lucidity at the end of life, in cases where there has been no lucidity for months or years. Terminal lucidity is not a brain dysfunction – it is the opposite: sudden resumption of normal cognitive function in the hours before death.

Second, there are DBV cases that demonstrate the DKD (didn't know they were dead) phenomenon that we saw with NDEs, ADCs, and mediumship. Some people have a DBV in which they see a person greeting them from the "other side" who they did not know was dead. They thought the person was alive, but unbeknownst to them, the person recently passed over. We ask the same question here that we asked with DKD cases in other areas: if a

DBV is just a hallucination, why is the person hallucinating a person on the "other side" whom they believe to be alive? That is a keenly perceptive hallucination.

Third, we also have reports of shared DBVs, in which a person at bedside – a relative or medical staff – *also* experience aspects of the DBV. This is similar to the shared NDE phenomena. These cannot be dismissed as hallucinations, because that is not how hallucinations work. And they can't be brushed off as the dysfunction of a dying brain, since the person at bedside is not even ill, much less dying. And yet they are sharing in the experience somehow.

I encourage you to look at the literature and make your own call. After having reading many DBV accounts, I believe that DBVs function as a sort of afterlife welcome committee, in which departed loved ones help ease the dying person's transition. I have provided some sources in the notes, if you would like to explore the subject further.[2]

DBV Researchers

Dr. Christopher Kerr is one of the leading researchers on DBVs. He has interviewed over 1400 people who've had DBVs. Dr. Kerr found that, among those who have DBVs, 72% "saw deceased family members, friends, and animals/pets." What percentage of those 72% saw animals/pets is not clear, since Dr. Kerr groups them together with family members and friends (appropriately enough).

We saw earlier that approximately 15% of NDEs and ADCs involve animals. If we assume that same percentage applies here, that would mean 210 of those 1400 saw animals/pets in their DBV. Even if we assume it was only 10%, that would still be 140 cases.

The vast majority, of course, are unpublished. Dr. Kerr does report several cases featuring animals, though. Most of these involve children who see a beloved pet who had passed away earlier. He states, "The message was the same, whether those who returned were animals or humans – that they were going to be okay, that they were not alone and that they were loved."

As we've seen in other areas, we see a parallel between "deceased" humans appearing in DBVs and "deceased" animals appearing in DBVs. These are not two different phenomena, just two aspects of the same phenomena. If you find the general human literature on DBVs persuasive, you can extend some of that credibility to the animal accounts. Please see Dr. Kerr's book for multiple examples of animals appearing in DBVs. [3]

Dr. Peter Fenwick is another physician who has studied DBVs intensively. In his book, *The Art of Dying*, Dr. Fenwick reports that animals who "have special significance for the dying person" appear in DBVs. Unfortunately, he does not provide specific examples. However, he is clear that companion animals do appear in some DBVs. [4]

What About Animals?

As usual, the literature is overwhelmingly focused on human beings. However, I did find 19 reports of animals featured in DBVs, supporting a belief in animal afterlife. There are hundreds of other unpublished reports (more on that in a moment), but I found 19 published ones.

Here are some examples.

Sparky

Niki Behrikis Shanahan reported the following account from a woman named Robin. Robin had a friend named Lou, who was dying of breast cancer.

Lou was attended by a nurse named Jan. Robin said Jan had a "strict religious upbringing" and that "Jan's firm stance was that animals do not have souls. Therefore, they could not go to Heaven, and they would not be there waiting to greet us."

After being in a coma for three weeks, Lou died. Jan attended her throughout the dying process. After Lou died, Jan called and told Robin that Lou had passed.

> *"But Jan didn't tell me the rest of the story for several weeks to come," Robin said. "It seems that on the night that Lou died, she awoke suddenly from her coma. Her eyes opened and she said one*

single, solitary word. Lou exclaimed in a quiet, weakened whisper, 'Sparky!' And then, just as suddenly as she had awakened, she died."

"None of Lou's family knew who 'Sparky' was. Not her husband of 45 years, not her grown children, not Jan, no one."

"A couple of weeks later, Jan got a call from Lou's family, asking her to please come to their home as soon as possible. It seemed they had something of great importance to show her. When Jan arrived, Lou's family greeted her with a smile, and then put something in Jan's hand. It was an old black and white picture of a little girl and a German Shepherd. On the back was hand-written in faded ink, 'Lou, age 10, and Sparky.'" [5]

The case has several interesting features:

1. Terminal lucidity: Lou wakes up from a long coma to say "Sparky," then dies.

2. No one knew who Sparky was. It took them weeks to figure it out. Lou had not mentioned Sparky to anyone; the dog had died 40 years ago. Jan could not have imagined Lou saying the name of an animal she never knew existed.

3. Jan had a strict religious upbringing and staunchly believed that animals did not have an afterlife. This event contradicts her religious beliefs. The fact that she waited three weeks before reporting it to Robin suggests to me that she was struggling with cognitive dissonance. This is a case of a skeptic having an experience that ran contrary to her worldview.

Dog Visitor

Scott Smith reported this case. Denise Dmytrasz was visiting her parents, because her father was ill and dying. Denise was in the kitchen, talking with her mother. Her father was lying in a bedroom down the hall.

Denise saw something out of the corner of her eye. She turned and saw a small dog walk past the doorway, heading toward the bedroom where her father lay. Denise turned to her mother and asked when they had gotten a dog. Her mother replied that they did not have a dog. They went looking through the house for the dog she had seen. They found nothing.

Her father died shortly after that. For a while, the strange dog visitor was a mystery. But they eventually learned that the dog looked like the spitz her father had when he was young. Denise said, "I believe the dog came to him to make it easier for the crossing over. I was surprised, because I never even knew my dad liked animals." [6]

The timing of the appearance is just prior to her father's passing, as is the case with most DBVs. We cannot explain it away as the hallucination of a dying brain, expectation, or wishful thinking, because Denise is not ill, and she has no reason to hallucinate an animal she never knew existed.

Czar

Gary Rothstein reported this story. Steve was dying of cancer. His wife Darin said that, as Steve got closer to death, he began telling her he was seeing their dog, Czar, walking down the hallway. Czar had died four years earlier.

Darin said Steve reported seeing Czar on several occasions before he died. Once, Steve made sure they stepped out of Czar's way, so he could pass in the hall. Czar was a Great Dane and needed some room.

Darin said that these visits from Czar gave Steve great joy and comfort in his final hours. [7]

Those are a few examples of cases in which human beings have seen animals in DBVs. If you believe that DBVs represent glimpses into an afterlife, rather than brain dysfunction, then these constitute evidence for animals in the afterlife. I found 19 such cases in the published literature, and there are likely hundreds more unpublished.

Do Animals Have DBVs?

If people have DBVs, what about animals? When they are approaching death, do they have their own welcome committees? It's hard to know, because animals can't talk, but I found half a dozen suggestive reports. I find them intriguing and thought you might, too.

Snowy

Vernon Neppe, MD, PhD, is a behavioral neurologist and neuropsychiatrist. He's a smart fellow. Dr. Neppe reported this experience, involving his dog, Snowy, who was very ill. She had lapsed into a coma.

Dr. Neppe reported:

> At about 7 pm, Snowy suddenly sat bolt upright, looked as if she was looking at an object very, very intensively and following that object with her eyes and her head moving from side to side. If a dog could smile, she was smiling. You could see there was a certain happiness radiating from her. She

began to wag her tail. Within seconds, she then plopped down and went back into coma. A short time later, Snowy died. [8]

There were multiple witnesses – Dr. Neppe, his wife, and his two adult children. All of them agreed on what they had seen. Snowy's behavior is very similar to a terminal lucidity DBV. The dog comes out of a coma, appears to be happily interacting with an unseen object or entity, and then lapses back into a coma and dies a short time later. That is very reminiscent of how human terminal lucidity DBVs happen in humans.

Little Meg

Here is another example, this one reported by William Thone.

Mr. Thone had three horses: Little Meg, Dan, and Beauty. Little Meg died first. Afterwards, Mr. Thone reported seeing Little Meg grazing with Dan and Beauty several times.

Years later, Mr. Thone was talking with Beauty, while Dan, who was ill at the time, was elsewhere. Then Mr. Thone heard a "shrill, wild neigh that could come only from Meg." When he followed the sound, he could see Little Meg standing beside Dan. The two horses turned and galloped away. "I listened to their fading hoofbeats and knew I had not imagined it," he said.

A few minutes later, some other men came in and announced that Dan had just died. The men had heard the other horse call, too, although they had not seen Meg. They said Dan died just as they hear the other horse call. Mr. Thorne said, "When you live with animals, you know their voices. I knew it was Meg's voice we had heard."   He saw her standing with Dan and galloping off as well. [9]

Later, it was Beauty's turn to cross over. Mr. Thone said something similar happened on this occasion, too. He was awakened at 2:30 a.m. by a horse call. He put on his boots and raincoat and went out to the barnyard to investigate.

"There in the light stood Little Meg, plainly silhouetted against the lighter, larger shape of Dan. Both were looking at the south gate, which was out of my line of vision. Meg threw up her head, tossed in in the old familiar way, and gave the rousing welcoming neigh I knew so well. Suddenly Beauty appeared at her side, and the three horses whirled and disappeared into the darkness."

Mr. Thone walked over to the area where they had been looking and switched on the lights. He found Beauty's body, lying in a mud puddle, still warm but lifeless.

Unless Mr. Thone is just fabricating this whole story, it is difficult to explain away as hallucination. They are DKD cases. Mr. Thorne does not know that the horses are dead when he sees them.

The stories also resemble what reportedly happens when human beings have DBVs – deceased loved ones (in this case, old horse friends) show up to help ease the transition. When it came time for one horse to pass, the others were there to help escort that horse over.

———————

Do animals have DBVs? We can't say with certainty, because animals cannot tell us verbally about their experiences. But these cases are at least suggestive of the possibility. And if human beings can have DBVs, why couldn't animals?

DBV Wrap Up

I found 19 case reports of animals appearing in human DBVs, and then six other cases suggesting that animals may have DBVs themselves. If you'd like to read more, check the notes. [10]

As usual, this number represents just a fraction of the total reports. We learned from Dr. Kerr that the majority of these cases go unpublished; Dr. Kerr probably has at least a hundred of them himself, and he is just one researcher. There are doubtless many more reports scattered about the internet, which I did not include.

We reviewed cases with corroborating features – DKD ("didn't know they were dead") cases, an appearance to someone who staunchly disbelieved in animal afterlife, DBV appearances of animals that no one knew even existed, and shared DBVs.

DBVs featuring animals parallel DBVs featuring human beings. In both cases, a loved one appears, the appearance is greeted with joy, and death follows shortly. In both cases, the DBV seems designed to help ease the transition. The fact that in one case, it is a human, and in the other case, an animal, does not seem to matter. They are two aspects of the same process. This has been the case with every phenomenon we have examined.

To the degree that you find the general DBV literature persuasive evidence for human survival, then you can transfer some of that credibility to the animal reports. That is, your appreciation for what the general literature shows helps inform how you see these cases. In my view, DBVs are another piece of evidence that animals have an afterlife.

Perhaps, when your time comes to cross over, animals will be part of your afterlife welcome committee.

Chapter 11

Ghost Reports

Many people giggle at the mention of ghosts, but ghosts (or "apparitions," if you prefer) have been reported in every society on Earth, since the dawn of civilization. They have been reported across all societies, all educational levels, all social strata, all religions and no religion, across millennia.

That is not to say all ghost reports are valid. Many are hoaxes. Many are misperceptions. However, there is good evidence that at least some reports are valid (i.e., not merely a subjective, unverifiable phenomenon). Most people are not aware of that evidence. I cannot do justice to it here, because the literature is too vast. If you would like to explore it, I've left some recommendations below. [1]

It is helpful to have some familiarity with the general literature, because that affects your view of the animal ghost reports that follow. I realize I have made this point several times. Pardon my repetition, but it's important. If you lack an appreciation of the general literature, it is easy to giggle and dismiss these reports as far-fetched nonsense. But if you understand that the general literature contains some valid cases, then you will be better disposed to consider evidence that you wouldn't otherwise.

"Ghosts are a part of our world. If you don't believe in them, that's because you haven't personally met one or read the literature about them." - Stafford Betty, PhD [2]

By the way, if you think that believing in ghosts is weird or fringe, think again. A 2019 IPSOS poll suggested that 46% of Americans believe in ghosts. That figure is up from 32% in 2005, which in turn was up from a previous figure of 25% in 1990. [3] In other words, belief in ghosts has nearly doubled in 30 years, at least in the United States. To be sure, popularity is no index of truth. Popular beliefs are often false. But people are much more open to belief in ghosts today than they were only a couple of decades ago. So if you decide to entertain that belief, don't feel weird.

I found a total of 55 animal ghost accounts in the published literature. As usual, this is just a small sample of the actual number of reports. I am aware, for example, that the Society for Psychical Research (SPR) has massive, multi-volume works containing thousands of human ghost reports. How many of those contain animals sightings? Who knows. Hundreds, I would guess, although I admit it is just a guess, because I haven't read those volumes myself. "Ghost hunting" is a popular hobby these days, so there are plenty of animal ghost sightings posted on the internet as well, which I did not gather up.

Ghosts vs. ADCs

In my opinion, ghosts and ADCs are two different phenomena. I discussed ADCs in earlier chapters, and I will discuss ghost reports in this one.

I should clarify this point, because some writers in this area use the terms interchangeably. They may call something a "ghost," when I think the better label is ADC. This can contribute to confusion. The confusion is not intentional; it's just a historical accident. The term "ADC" was only coined a couple of decades ago. Before that, every visual appearance was lumped together as an "apparition" or a "ghost," without much distinction. But ghosts and ADCs are different. It is helpful to sort this out.

Here are the main differences between ghosts and ADCs:

Emotional connection: In an ADC, there is usually an emotional connection between the experiencer and the "deceased" individual (human or animal). With a ghost report, the person seeing a ghost is usually a stranger, with no emotional connection to the figure being seen.

People vs. places: ADCs are usually connected to particular people – primarily, the people that the "deceased" individual (human or animal) is bonded with. Ghosts, on the other hand, seem more tied to places than to people.

Timing: ADCs usually happen shortly after death – within hours, days, or weeks of passing. Ghost sightings, on the other hand, can occur years, decades, and in some cases even centuries after the death of the individual.

Aftereffects: After experiencing an ADC, most people feel comfort and reassurance. After encountering a ghost, many people feel unsettled, disturbed, or even frightened.

Process Differences: ADCs seem to be communications "on the way out," like sending a letter while boarding a plane, before flying off to another country. Ghosts seem to be something different. In the literature, ghosts are often referred to as "earth-bound" entities, perhaps "stuck" in some sense. ADCs are not.

Trauma: Ghost reports are often associated with some sort of traumatic or violent death. That is rare in ADC reports.

Because of those differences, I consider ADCs and ghosts two different phenomena, and I discuss them separately.

While we are on the subject of ghosts, I should make the distinction between an "intelligent haunt" and a "residual haunt." In an intelligent haunt, the ghost interacts with observers in a way that suggests an intelligent presence. It may respond to prompts, for example. In a residual haunt, there is no interaction. The ghost is more like a visual recording that plays over and over, the same way each time.

I found both intelligent and residual types in the animal literature, but most of them were of the intelligent, interactive sort.

―――――――――

Animal Ghosts

Many of the 55 cases were of the "simple encounter" type we saw with ADCs – events witnessed by one person, without any additional factors, beyond the person's word, that would add to its credibility. In these cases, you basically have a choice of either believing that the person is reporting accurately, and that their report reflects something real (i.e., evidence of an afterlife), or else you dismiss them as being either dishonest or mistaken somehow.

However, many of the cases involved multiple witnesses. Cases with multiple witness are harder to write off as lies or misperceptions. If two different people see a ghost on two different occasions, and they both give a similar description of the ghost, what then? Are they both lying? Both hallucinating?

I'll share a few cases like this.

Ghost Cat

Journalist Arthur Myers reported on the ghost of a yellow and white cat, who repeatedly appeared in the small bedroom of a house in New Jersey. The cat would always appear on the same bed. The woman who owned the house did not know the cat. No one was able to identify the cat.

Several different people saw the cat at different times, and all of them gave the same description. In addition to those people, many other people said they felt the cat's fur, while sitting on the bed. The woman who owned the house replaced the bed four times, thinking that the cat might be linked to the bed somehow, but that did no good. The ghost cat continued to make an appearance on the new furniture.

The house became fairly well known, attracting visitors and parapsychological investigators. Hundreds of people reported feeling warm spots where the cat had lain. There were many witnesses. Sightings extended over many years. [4]

The Headless Cat

Elliot O'Donnell reported this case. It's a strange one, but what the heck – everybody loves a good ghost story.

The account comes from an attorney who had just moved into a new house in Manchester with his wife. The attorney described himself as "stodgy and unimaginative" and his wife as "the most practical and matter-of-fact woman you would meet in a day's march."

Shortly after moving in, the attorney said that his wife woke him up, calling his attention to a series of loud screeches, growls and snarls coming from the landing at the top of the stairs. He got up and searched that area, but he found no sign of anything. All the doors and windows were closed and locked. They had no pets.

The next night, he was climbing the stairs and felt a "rush of icy cold air" go past him. He looked down and saw "two big red eyes" staring at him from below the banister.

A couple of weeks later, their children came running into their room, screaming that a dog had trapped a cat in the spare room, and it was "tearing it to pieces." When they reached the room, he heard "the most appalling pandemonium of screeches and snarls" from behind the door – "as if some dog had got hold of a cat by the neck and was shaking it to death." They opened the door, and the sounds abruptly stopped. The room was empty.

A week later, their cook resigned. She said she had been disturbed by "screeches outside my door, which sound like a cat, but which I know can't be a cat, as there is no cat in the house." The cook said:

"Something heavy sprang right on top of me and gave a loud growl in my ear. That finished me mum. I wouldn't go through what I suffered again for fifty pounds. I've got palpitations even now. I would rather go without my month's wages than sleep in that room another night."

A week afterwards, the attorney returned home to find his wife in a panic. She told him she had heard a "very pathetic mew" coming from under the sofa. She looked under the sofa, but she didn't see anything. Again, she heard the mewing. This time, she heard something crawl out from under the sofa. She still couldn't see anything.

"Then," she said, "something sprang upon me and dug its claws into my knees. I looked down, and to my horror and distress, perceived, standing on its hindlegs, pawing my clothes, a large tabby cat, without a head – the neck terminating in a mangled stump."

A week later, the attorney heard a loud noise in the hall.

"[It was] as if a dog had pounced on a cat. And the next moment, a large tabby, with the head hewn

away as Delia had described, rushed up to me and tried to spring on my shoulders." [5]

After all of that commotion, the attorney decided to investigate the history of the property. Eventually, he discovered that, 12 years earlier, a married couple had lived there. They had spoiled their son, Arthur, "even to the extent of encouraging him in acts of cruelty." To amuse Arthur, the parents would buy him rats for his dog to kill. On one occasion, they got him a stray cat. The dog mangled the cat badly, and then Arthur killed it.

The attorney suggested that, perhaps that would explain the appearances. He and his family were seeing the ghost of the poor cat and hearing re-enactments of its torture. As I mentioned earlier, ghost reports are often associated with violent or traumatic death.

Admittedly, that is a strange case. Here are some features that add to its credibility, though:

- o Multiple witnesses – six of them, in fact (the attorney, his wife, his brother-in-law, the children, and the cook). All of them saw related phenomena at different times.

- o The attorney describes himself as "stodgy and unimaginative" and his wife as "very practical and matter of fact." They do not seem prone to imaginative flights of fancy.

- o The sightings occur over an extended period of time.

- o Historical data, uncovered after the fact, is consistent with the appearances.

Ghost Dog

This account comes from journalist Scott Smith.

A ghost dog was seen by six people on several different occasions. All six witnesses agreed on the dog's appearance. They said it was two feet high, with black body, tan eyebrows and paws, short ears, a curly tail, and large, dark eyes.

Two people saw the dog disappearing through a solid door. One woman noted that that when she saw the dog, "I remember an alteration of my surroundings, with everything having a slightly hazy iridescence."

The dog was a stranger to everyone. No one recognized who the dog was. The appearances all occurred at the same house. There was no dog in the house. [6]

So, we have six people, all seeing a ghost dog on different occasions, all in the same house, and all of them giving matching descriptions of the dog. This is very difficult to write off as hallucination or misperception.

If you would like to read other animal ghost reports, including multiple witness accounts, I have listed sources below. [7]

Ghost Wrap Up

It is fine to retain some skepticism about this stuff. I am naturally skeptical, so I find some of this stuff a little hard to believe sometimes, despite knowing that the general literature on ghosts/apparitions contains many persuasive accounts.

In this small subset of animal reports, there are plenty of multiple witness accounts, which are difficult to wave away as hallucination, misperception, or wishful thinking. In some cases, we have six or more people, all providing matching descriptions of the ghost animal, with multiple sightings of the same ghost over an extended period of time. In many cases, they do not know the identity of the animal being seen. Unless you assume all of them are hallucinating, all of them are mistaken, or all of them are lying, then you will find it difficult to explain them away in ordinary, naturalistic terms.

Even if many ghost reports are misperception or imagination run amok, that still doesn't mean they all are. All ghost accounts don't have to be valid. In order to provide evidence of animal afterlife, just one account needs to be valid.

Are they all mistaken? Are they all lying? Are they all just hallucinating the same figment of their imagination?

Chapter 12

Out of Body Experiences

In an Out of Body Experience (OBE), a person sees their body from an external perspective. In the typical OBE, the person is above their body, at a height of about four to six feet, looking down on it. In some OBEs, the person travels to other locations – for instance, to other parts of the hospital, back home, or to visit someone else. And in the more elaborate OBEs, the person engages in astral travel to other dimensions, including the afterlife.

Skeptics dismiss OBEs as hallucination or imaginative fantasy. However, there is reason to believe that at least some OBE reports are valid. For instance, the authors of *The Self Does Not Die* review over 100 cases of veridical OBEs during NDEs.[1] Veridical OBEs are cases in which the person reports information that he/she could not have known through normal means, and the information is later verified to be accurate.

Dr. Kenneth Ring has also documented 30 cases of blind people who reported veridical OBEs during NDEs.[2] Some of these people were born blind; they had never seen anything in their entire life. Yet they reported OBEs during an NDE in which they experienced full visual perception, seeing things in clarity and color.

They were also able to describe visual elements in the surgical environment – that the surgeon had grey eyes, wore glasses, and was overweight, for example, or how the instruments looked and were laid out. When these people recovered and reported their observations, the medical team verified them as accurate. Sometimes, the reports concerned activities in other locations outside the OR; these, too, were verified as accurate.

These are people who are blind, sometimes blind from birth, often clinically "dead" at the time of the NDE, able to see things clearly while in an OBE state, and able to describe visual aspects of the environment accurately, both within and outside the surgical room.

If you would like to read about evidence supporting the validity of some OBEs, I have listed sources below. [3]

Animals in Astral Travel

For our purposes, we will restrict ourselves to OBE reports in which the experiencer reports travel to an afterlife dimension. I will refer to these as astral travel reports.

Granted, we do not have the same level of support for the validity of these cases as we do for more typical OBE cases, which involve the normal, physical realm. It is easy enough to validate reports about the normal, physical realm by simply checking the facts in that realm. For instance, does the surgeon match the description given by the blind person in her OBE – is the surgeon overweight, with grey eyes and glasses? However, as I'm sure you can appreciate, validating an OBE of the afterlife is a bit more challenging. That would require checking the reported observations with the objective facts in the afterlife. But of course, we don't have access to the objective facts in the afterlife.

These reports do not lack all support, though. First, as we have just noted, we have support for the credibility of some OBEs, at least those confined to the normal, physical realm. This can perhaps give us some confidence in OBEs that travel outside that realm. At least we know that the base phenomena is not simply imagination, dissociative experience, or hallucination.

Second, we can look for consistency in these astral travel reports. Even if we cannot objectively verify those observations by consulting the afterlife, the correlations between those observations are some evidence of the reality that they describe. Even if we cannot verify the details of some remote city in Algiers, if dozens of visitors all describe a similar location, then we can have some confidence that such a city really exists. It is not proof, of course, but the correspondence among reports furnishes some reason to grant those reports credibility, just as correspondence among a dozen witnesses confers credibility on those reports.

In other words, consistency among astral travel reports suggests that they may be describing a real place. If these astral travelers were all just dreaming or engaged in some kind of self-induced fantasy, then their observations should vary widely, just as dreams and imaginative fantasies do. Yet astral travel reports often have a correspondence with each other, as if the visitors are describing a real place, albeit from different vantage points.

As always, the general OBE literature focuses primarily on human beings. However, I managed to find 21 reports of animals appearing in the afterlife, in the form of astral travel reports.

Here are four examples.

The Forest

Robert Monroe is probably the most famous OBE astral traveler. Monroe has written several books describing his astral travels. He also established the Monroe Institute, which trains people to consciously initiate OBEs.

Monroe described several encounters with animals in afterlife dimensions. Here is one example.

> *The walk back along the path through the forest is filled with greetings. A squirrel on a low branch looks down and chatters. A bottle-green fly lands on a hand and enjoys gentle back-stroking with a finger. Three turkeys stand aside and watch the passage curiously but without wariness. A gray fox wanders onto the path and sits down, undecided as to whether to pay his respects. A thrush glides down, settles on a shoulder, and chirps softly into an ear until the edge of the forest is reached.* [4]

Lions and Lambs

Harold Sharp reported about a dozen astral travel OBEs in which he saw animals in the afterlife. In one example, he encountered "a friend with his raven, and a couple of dogs which I had not met before" as well as a boy with a rabbit.

Later, Harold reported seeing this:

> A perfect menagerie of animals, playing in absolute freedom. Further afield, I found lions and tigers, foxes, elephants, monkeys and meditative camels, and tropical birds of brilliant color. Indeed, every living creature you could think of. The prophesy that the lion should lie down with the lamb was no fable. In this land without fear, harming instincts seemed to be non-existent. [5]

———————

Monroe Institute

Bill Schul conducted workshops at the Monroe Institute. Bill stated that many of the institute trainees would see animals in their astral travels. However, these mentions were often "an afterthought" to the trainees. If specific questions about animals were not asked, the trainees would not mention them, so the presence of animals could easily have been missed. That sort of oversight is similar to what we saw in other areas (e.g., NDEs), where animals are an afterthought. If you don't ask about something, you often won't hear about it. Thus, their presence is under-reported.

Bill added, however, that whenever animals *were* seen in an afterlife OBE, the attitude was always one of "complete acceptance" that, well *of course* animals exist in the afterlife. As you will recall, this is the same "of course" attitude expressed by evidential mediums.

One of Bill's friends had many OBEs. Bill asked him if he saw animals on the other side. His friend replied, "Oh yes, I often see animals there, sometimes with other animals, such as several dogs playing or running together. Or they may be with a person. It isn't unusual for me to see someone romping with a dog or holding and stroking a cat."

His friend also reported encountering his old dog, Flip, who had died several months earlier. He said, "He was really excited to see me. We wagged his tail and kept jumping against me. I petted him, talked to him for quite a spell, and never doubted the reality of the experience." [6]

———————

Swedenborg

Emmanuel Swedenborg was a scientist, inventor, and theologian who lived in the 19th century. He wrote books on the afterlife and included reports of his own visions and astral travels. Here is a description from one of those OBEs:

> *"I looked around and saw birds of gorgeous colors. Some were flying; some were sitting on trees; and some were down in the meadow, plucking the petals off roses. Among the birds were also doves and swans. Then I saw, not far from me, flocks of sheep and lambs and of kids and nanny-goats. Around the flocks I saw herds of cattle and calves, as well as camels and mules."* [7]

————————

Ninja

One more brief example, this one from Scott Smith. Smith relates this account from a woman named Adrienne.

Adrienne had an astral travel OBE in which she interacted with her deceased cat, Ninja. Adrienne said that Ninja's "second body was as real and tactile as if he were alive." She added, "I learned more about the universe in those few moments than all the books, lectures, and teachers in my lifetime. I now know there is a life after death for animals as well as humans." [8]

————————

I found 21 cases of astral travel reports featuring animals. I confess that I did not read the OBE literature thoroughly, so there is no doubt I missed many other animal reports. I know that many people, from the dabblers to the proficient, engage in astral travel. There must be dozens if not hundreds of animal reports that I did not find, either on the internet or in print. So, 21 is just a small sample. It will have to do.

In my view, OBEs provide some additional support for belief in animal afterlife. If you would like to read further accounts, please see the sources in the notes for this chapter.

Chapter 13

Instrumental Transcommunication

Instrumental transcommunication (ITC) is a broad term that covers any form of purported communication from the afterlife that comes through electronic or physical media. ITC includes electronic voice phenomena (EVP), communications through the telephone, radio, computer, or photographs.

I am not aware of any animals coming through via the telephone, radio, or computer. Those cases may be out there; I admit I am not as familiar with this area as I would like to be, so I may just be unaware of cases that do exist. Or maybe dogs just don't know our phone number.

I will confine my discussion here to EVP and spirit photography. For those interested in exploring ITC more broadly, I've listed some sources in the notes. [1]

Electronic Voice Phenomena (EVP)

Electronic Voice Phenomena (EVP) are discernable voices that appear on audio recording when no one else is around. For example, a woman may sit quietly, alone, with a voice recorder running. She asks to hear from any spirits that may be present. She asks some questions, in the hope of prompting a response.

When she is listening, she hears nothing, but when she plays back the recording, she hears, among the white noise, snippets that sound like words being spoken. Some may sound like replies to the questions she posed.

EVPs vary in quality. Most are faint and difficult to make out. Some, a minority, are clear and distinct. The main danger in this area is pareidolia, which is imagining meaningful patterns in random noise. Our brains are pattern-seeking machines, and they will sometimes impose patterns where there are none. We can "hear" human voices in white noise or "see" patterns in random images. Our brains "see" and "hear" patterns when there are none.

I believe that pareidolia is the likely explanation for many reported EVPs, especially those of low quality. I have heard some of these EVPs and been unimpressed. Although the person reporting the EVP insists that specific words can be heard, I can only do so by straining my imagination; all I hear is random fluctuations.

However, not all crows are black, and not all EVPs are low-quality. I have heard some high-quality EVPs, where pareidolia could easily be ruled out. The words were clear and distinct. In addition, some of these cases involve remarkable timing in question and response – a specific question is asked, and a specific reply immediately follows. In those cases, it is hard to escape the impression that a conversation is taking place. In some cases, the speaker will identify himself or herself as deceased, then go on to discuss aspects of the afterlife. In most cases, though, EVPs are rather brief.

I have listed some sources below, if you would like to explore the topic of EVPs further. [2]

———————

Animal EVPs

Do animals show up in EVP, thus giving some evidence of animal afterlife? Yes, they do. I found about a dozen such reports. I counted multiple EVPs of the same animal as a single instance, to keep my counts conservative.

For several reasons, I am confident that this number (12) is a severe underestimate of the actual number of EVPs featuring animals. First, I am not very conversant with the EVP literature; it just hasn't been of particular interest to me, so I haven't read it in depth. No doubt there are many published reports featuring animals of which I am unaware. Second, there are many EVP practitioners (it has become quite popular), but not many write books. These people are gathering auditory evidence, after all, and that doesn't translate well to print. You really have to hear it for yourself. Given the large number of EVP practitioners, I assume there are hundreds of unpublished incidents of animals appearing in EVPs. Third, EVPs will sometimes get posted in various places on the internet. I did not include those sources.

Here are a few examples of what I found in the published literature.

Muffin

Martha Copeland had a daughter, Cathy, who died. When she was still alive, Cathy had a dog named Muffin. Muffin was her close companion for 17 years. Shortly after Cathy died, so did Muffin.

Martha has a recording of Cathy saying, "Mama, I have Muffin," followed by a bark. At other times, Martha has also heard Cathy calling for her other dogs, Shishi and Grete, who are both deceased.

Cathy also had a pet rat named Elainey, who was still alive when Martha recorded Cathy singing, "Elainey, Elainey, I miss my rat Elainey!" Weeks later, Cathy indicated that she was coming to help Elainey transition. Elainey died a short time later. [3]

Getting on Spirit's Nerves

Lisa Butler, who had been communicating via EVP for some time, became worried about the fate of animals during a natural disaster that struck her area. Lisa asked her contact on the other side about the animals. The reply came back, "Animals also survive." The EVP added that many people on the other side work to rescue the animals and help bring them over. "They continue," the voice said. "Nothing that lives is ever lost."

Lisa said that, eventually, she got on the spirit's nerves, because she kept asking the same question about the animals every night. The spirits would always give reassuring replies. After she had asked the same question seven nights in a row, "a loud, frustrated voice replied, 'Stop with the animals! They are all right!'" Lisa said she was embarrassed; "I realized I had become as irritating as a two-year old who incessantly repeats the same question." [4]

If you would like to read other examples of animals appearing in EVPs, please see the notes.[5]

Spirit Photography

In what is sometimes known as "spirit photography," images appear on unexposed photographic film, and the images closely resemble deceased people. In the better cases, the film is carefully stored under lock and key, unexposed to external light or input, and then spirits are invited to imprint an image on the film. The images that result from this process can sometimes be remarkably clear.

Sonia Rinaldi is one of the primary researchers in this area. You can see some of the images she has captured by going to the link provided in the notes.[6] Among them you will see an image of a dog. The identity of this particular dog is unknown. In many other cases, Sonia has gotten images of "deceased" dogs and other animals whose identity can be established.

People working in this area do not tend to publish many books. In part, that may be because spirit photography does not translate very well to text. You really have to see it. You can try printing the photographs, but that will raise the cost of publishing, and unless you have a big publisher behind you (which these people do not), the resolution of your photos will suffer.

In the published literature, I found 33 reported cases of animals showing up in spirit photography. Unfortunately, in most cases, the images were not reproduced in the book, so we only have text descriptions. As usual, this is an underestimate. Sonia Rinaldi reports many cases of animals showing up in her work. There are many other cases scattered about the internet, not included here.

Here are some examples.

At the Gravestone

Vincent and Margaret Gaddis reported this account from Anne Elizabeth Blochin.

Mrs. Blochin owned a pet cemetery called Happy Woodland. One day, during an unveiling ceremony for a central monument, a visiting photographer took a photo of a grave marker. The photographer was only interested in the gravestone. At the time of the photo, she saw no dogs in the area.

When the photographer developed the negative, though, "she was amazed to see, clearly defined in the picture, the figure of a dog lying at the foot of the grave." The photographer sent a copy of the photo to Mrs. Blochin, who confirmed that it was "the undeniable likeness of a dog, although there were no living dogs in the cemetery at the time."

Mrs. Blochin showed the photo to the owners of the grave. She said:

> *"They immediately recognized it as that of their pet, a beloved small mongrel. He had been buried there some months before. That this might not be thought the power of mere suggestion, they submitted several photographs of the dog in life, which show a resemblance so striking as to be remarkable."* [7]

———————

Doggie in the Window

Scott Smith relates this account, from Ray Tweedy and Leon Thompson.

Ray and Leon had a dog, Brutus, who they loved very much. During the Christmas season, they would always hang a Christmas wreath in their front window. When Brutus was alive, he would sit and look at the wreath for long periods of time.

The Christmas after Brutus died, the men took a picture of the wreath from outside the house. When they got the photo developed, "There was Brutus looking out the window. You can see the rings around his eyes and nose and even the flopped ear on the right side." [8]

――――――――

Other Cases

Sylvia Barbanell recounts eight cases of animals in spirit photography.[9] For example, she said that one photo showed "the clear and distinct likeness" of a terrier who had passed away. Another photo showed the image of a deceased dog, lying in his favorite spot.

Slyvia Barbanell attested that she had examined all of the photos and in each case, she found them persuasive. She said that the images clearly resembled how the deceased animal looked when alive. She also discussed how alternative explanations had been ruled out in several cases. Please see her book for further discussion.

――――――――

If you would like to read about other cases where "deceased" animals appear in photographs, see the notes for sources.[10]

ITC Wrap Up

In the published literature, I found 21 OBE reports and 33 photographs featuring animals, providing support for belief in animal afterlife.   For various reasons described earlier, these are significant underestimates of the actual number of cases.

What you make of these cases is, of course, up to you. Personally, I take a somewhat cautious stance, in part because I am not as familiar with these areas as I am with others.   However, I have seen enough to know that there is something genuine going on here – it isn't just a matter of misperception, pareidolia, imaginative fantasy, or hallucination.   Some OBEs are clearly veridical.   There are some high-quality EVPs, with remarkable content.   Sonia Rinaldi and others are producing some very impressive work with spirit photography. Beyond that, there is the field of ITC more broadly, which contains some persuasive evidence.

Taken together, there is just too many strong cases to dismiss it all as fraud, pareidolia, misperception, or the like. I don't think these are all black crows. There are too many good cases, produced by reputable people, to blithely wave them all away like that.

ITC cases support a belief in animal afterlife. They attest that there is an afterlife, and that animals are a part of it.

Chapter 14

God's Character

Some people believe in a God who is the source of and foundation for the universe. Some people don't. If you don't, you might want to skip this chapter. It will probably seem irrelevant to you. I am taking a belief in that sort of God as a starting point for this argument.

I am not arrogant enough to assume I know who/what "God" is. I am not using the term in a narrow, religious sense. If you have difficulty with the term "God," feel free to substitute words like "source," "intelligence," or "force." I am also going to use the traditional masculine pronoun, "he," rather than repeating the cumbersome "he/she/it."

I know we get in trouble when we try to assign attributes to God. However, since an attribute-free God is no different than no God at all, I will say this much. I think God, whoever he is, has some of the following attributes:

- o Intelligence
- o Love
- o Goodness
- o Fairness

207

This is not an exhaustive description, clearly. And I make no claims to be a theologian. This is just my opinion. However, I'm not pulling it out of thin air. The characteristic of intelligence is a logical inference, and the other attributes are common beliefs held by most theistic religions.

Here is a question: If you believe that a God like that exists, then does it make sense that he would create an afterlife for humans but not animals? If God is highly intelligent and basically good, fair, and loving, would he bar animals from the afterlife?

I don't think so. To give human beings an afterlife but send animals to the grave would be a contradiction of each of those characteristics. I'll explain why.

––––––––––––

Intelligence

Fair to say, I think, that God is a bright fellow. Anyone who is the source and foundation of all that exists possesses an intellect far beyond our puny human ones. As one illustration of this, astronomer Hugh Ross compared the level of fine-tuning evident in one aspect of chemistry to the most accurately-tuned machines built by humans. Based on that comparison, Dr. Ross stated, "God must be at least a hundred trillion times more capable than human beings."[1] And that chemical fine-tuning is just one aspect of how the universe is finely tuned for life; there are dozens of others. If you take Ross's calculation at face value, then God is at least a hundred trillion times smarter than we are.

Would a God that smart give humans an afterlife but not animals? Granted, I'm using my puny human intellect to answer that question, but I don't think so. Here is why.

I'm a retired psychologist, so I'm going to use cognitive-behavioral therapy (CBT) principles to illustrate this. You could just as well use philosophical principles, but I'm using what I know best. In CBT, therapists work to identify "cognitive distortions" – thinking errors that contribute to emotional distress. Cognitive distortions are associated with depression, anxiety, and most emotional troubles. A CBT therapist works with clients to identify and correct these thinking errors.

Google for yourself "top ten cognitive distortions," and you will get a bunch of lists. On every list, you will find a cognitive distortion called "all-or-nothing thinking" (or "black-and-white thinking). In other circles, this might be called "binary" or "dichotomous" thinking.

If we are engaged in the cognitive distortion called all-or-nothing thinking, we things in two polar extremes, with nothing in between. Things are either good or bad, not a mix. You're either a success or a failure, not a success in some ways but a failure in others.

Please notice: this is exactly the kind of thinking we are supposed to believe *God* engages in, when he decides that people get an afterlife but animals do not. God supposedly starts by saying, "Either you are a human being or an animal," although we know that human beings *are* animals. God supposedly then goes on to say, "Human beings have reason, but animals do not" and "Human beings have moral sense, but animals do not" – both of which are untrue (see the chapter, Do Animals Qualify for the Afterlife?) – in fact, these attributes exist on a continuum, not in an all-or-nothing fashion.   And God then concludes by saying, "Human beings get into heaven, but animals do not." One type of animal gets it all, the other type gets nothing.

Are we to believe that a supremely intelligent God – a God who is a hundred trillion times smarter than we are – would be engaged in a common thinking error like this? Something that makes the list of Top Ten Cognitive Distortions (indeed, it is often the first one listed)?

Which is more likely:

1. That a God of infinite intelligence, facing an incredibly consequential decision that would affect the eternal lives of billions of creatures, got stuck in a thinking error that most human beings can spot easily? Or,

2. That the all-or-nothing thinking here is *our* cognitive error, not God's.

_____

Love

When people speak of God, they often do so in terms of love. Other words would be care or compassion. Love is a central attribute of God's character. God loves his creation; he cares about it. Some people say God *is* love.

Two points.

First, if God loves his creation – and his creation certainly includes animals – then would it be loving to snuff out their spirits at death, when he could just as well give them an afterlife as he does for humans? Is that loving? If you had the power to save the life of a friend, and you didn't use it, how much love do you have for that friend?

If God is loving, why would he snuff out all the souls of animals at physical death? Is that love? Is it loving to let animals rot in the grave, when you have the power to do otherwise?

Second point. If God is loving – more still if he *is* love -- how can he turn his back on love? Love is present between animals, and it also is present between people and animals. If love is one of God's most important attributes, why would he throw love in the trash?

If God is loving, would he not respect and value love in others? To discard or disrespect love would be to contradict his own nature and system of meaning. Yet this is what some people believe – that God would throw the love between animals, and our love for them, into the trash bin.

I cannot believe that. If there is a God who is loving, he would not discard love.

Goodness

Most people who believe in God would agree that God is good. A god who is not good would hardly be a god worth believing in.

Goodness implies beneficence and benevolence; if an action is benevolent and beneficial, we call it "good." If God granted you an afterlife but not your pet, would that be a good act? Would that be evidence of goodness?

I don't think so. That would not be benevolent or beneficial. I love my dogs, and my relationships with them are very important to me. If God consigns my dogs to the dust heap, he is treating something I value deeply like it means nothing. If a human being treated my dogs like trash, I would be angry, because that behavior is wrong; it is bad. And to deprive my dogs of an afterlife is certainly not beneficial to the dogs.

God cannot be both good (benevolent) and also deprive animals of an afterlife while granting it to humans. That would be a contradiction of his character.

Here is another angle on the subject. I don't buy the traditional conception of heaven and hell, but even if I did, I wouldn't want a heaven that lacked animals. Imagine that for a moment: a heaven with only people, no animals. Maybe you have a few angels fluttering about, but otherwise, it's all people – people, people, people, everywhere you look. No dogs, cats, birds, frogs, horses, fish, rabbits, mice, bears, otters, pigs, monkeys, raccoons, or anything. People, people, people, everywhere, all the time.

I thought heaven was supposed to be heavenly? I don't know about you, but I'm a big introvert, and I wouldn't want to spend a week in a "heaven" like that, much less eternity. If God is good, he would not create a heaven that sucks. If heaven is heavenly, it must contain animals.

> If there are no dogs in heaven, then when I die, I want to go where they went.
>
> – Will Rogers

One more point. Think about how much goodness animals bring into your life. They bring affection, loyalty, and love. They bring health, laughter, and play. They bring connection, stimulation, and friendship.

If animals are the source of so much goodness, why would a good God exclude goodness from the afterlife? That would be a blatant contradiction of his character. If God is good, he would respect goodness and want to preserve it, not toss it away.

———————

Fairness

The last characteristic I'll talk about is a concern with fairness or justice. If God is concerned with fairness (as most theists believe), then would it make sense for him to give human beings an afterlife, but not give it to animals?

The afterlife is a pretty big gift. If God is fair, would he give that huge gift to humans, but not to animals? Animals are his children, too. Imagine that you had two children. If you gave one child a wonderful gift, and gave the other child nothing at all, would that be fair? One child gets eternal life, and the other gets death?

Unless you can provide strong justification for that, it would be blatantly unfair. Of course, some religions have tried to provide that justification. I hope I've made the case elsewhere that those justifications are unsupportable.

A God who is fair would not give an afterlife to human beings and give nothing to animals. That would be grossly unfair. It would contradict his character.

———————

In brief, the type of God I described – one who is intelligent, loving, good, and fair – would not give human beings an afterlife, but withhold it from animals. That would contradict his character in multiple ways. That's not who he is.

Chapter 15

Counting the Cases

Let's recap the evidence briefly, at least in terms of the numbers. When I searched the literature, I found the following:

- o 62 NDE reports of animal afterlife

- o An estimated 766 other NDE reports of animals in the afterlife in the nderf.org database (15% of total)

- o Hundreds of unpublished NDEs supporting animal afterlife in the files of one NDE researcher

- o 112 visual ADCs of animal afterlife

- o 55 auditory, 42 tactile, and 6 olfactory ADCs of animal afterlife

- o An estimated 280 other ADC accounts of animals in the afterlife on the adcrf.org website

- o 91 evidential mediumship accounts (providing specific, details they could not have known) of animal afterlife o All the mediums of which I am aware have stated that animals are a part of the afterlife

o A controlled scientific experiment supporting animal afterlife

o 25 physical mediumship accounts of animal afterlife

o An estimated hundreds of other physical mediumship accounts of animals in the afterlife contained in the Leslie Flint archives.

o 19 DBV reports of animal afterlife, with 6 reports suggesting animals themselves may have DBVs

o An estimated 210 other unpublished DBVs in the files of Dr. Chistopher Kerr, supporting animal afterlife

o 55 ghost reports of animal afterlife

o 21 OBEs featuring animals in the afterlife

o 12 EVPs and 33 spirit photographs supporting belief in animal afterlife

(Mostly) Limited to the Published Literature

In my search, I looked primarily at the published literature – i.e., books and articles. I will not claim to have made an exhaustive survey of that literature. I did what I could, but I am just one guy. I am sure there are things I missed.

There were some bits of the literature that I chose to exclude. For instance, the SPR has huge, multivolume tomes on apparitions, spanning thousands of pages. I could have obtained those volumes and then read through them until my eyes fell out, searching for ghost reports on animals. I chose not to do that. I am a mere mortal, with a staff of one (me). I did what I could.

I also left the internet alone, for the most part. The internet is a bottomless pit of websites and forums at least tangentially devoted to this sort of thing. I could have spent the rest of my life scouring the internet for ADCs, NDEs, and whatnot. I did not want to do that, so I didn't. I did make reference to a few of the main websites, but otherwise I left the internet out. I wanted to keep the project manageable and retain my sanity. But that means there are hundreds, probably thousands of internet reports that are not included here.

We also have to understand that *published* literature represents only the tip of the iceberg – most reports are unpublished. We know, for instance, that hundreds of unpublished NDEs of animal afterlife are in the file drawers of Dr. Milton Hadley of Cambridge. The same situation probably obtains for other NDE researchers as well. Realistically, we cannot expect them to publish hundreds of long narratives – no one would want to read that.

The same situation exists with DBVs. We know that hundreds of unpublished DBV accounts exist in one researcher's files, and the same situation is probably true for other researchers. In fact, the same situation probably exists in every area under consideration here. The published accounts will represent only a small fraction of the actual number of reported cases.

And the reported cases, whether published or not, represent only a small fraction of the actual number of *experiences*. People generally do not report their experiences, first because they are very personal; second because they do not want to expose themselves to potential ridicule; and third because most people simply aren't interested in doing so.

I should mention one other factor. We saw repeatedly, and to no one's surprise, that the afterlife literature is concerned first and foremost with human survival. Animals are an afterthought, if they are mentioned at all. For example, we saw that NDE researchers did not even think to ask about the presence of animals in NDEs. Unfortunately, when you are doing interview and questionnaire-based research, you will often not hear about what you fail to ask about.

All of that is to say: published cases represent only a small fraction of the actual number of cases. Just taking the published numbers alone, we have hundreds of cases providing evidence of animal afterlife. If we add in the cases which are either unpublished or posted on the internet, the number rises into the thousands.

We have now completed our survey of the evidence. In the next chapter, we will assess that evidence and decide what we think about it.

Chapter 16

Weighing the Evidence

Do animals have an afterlife? I've presented some evidence and arguments on that question. Now it's time for you to make an assessment, a judgment of your own. Where do you stand on the question? What do you think is the most likely answer? Do animals have an afterlife, or don't they?

I'll explain several different approaches you might take, a couple of things to consider, and then I'll leave you to your decision.

Approaches to the Question

I see six different approaches to weighing the evidence. There may be more, and you are welcome to use whatever approach you like, but these are the six that I see as options:

1. Personal experience
2. Scientific experiments
3. Courtroom standards
4. Intuition
5. Cumulative probability
6. Best explanation

Each approach has strengths and weaknesses. I will describe them for you. Then you can choose the approach(es) that best fit you. I would suggest using several approaches in combination, rather than just one.

Personal Experience

Personal experience can be very persuasive. If you have had a personal experience in this area (e.g., an ADC), then you may have decided the issue already, just based on that. Personal experiences can be convincing in a way that reading about others' experiences are not. It can also open your mind to other evidence.

The *lack* of personal experience can work the other way around. If you have never had a personal experience, despite having lost loved ones, you may be more skeptical of the reports of others' experiences. You may find their accounts hard to believe, because you haven't had an experience like that yourself.

Personal experience can be powerful, but it does have one serious disadvantage. You are giving an awful lot of authority to a single person to decide the question. Granted, that person is you – someone you know and presumably trust. But it is still just one person's experience, and we are all capable of fooling ourselves. It is wiser, I think, to consider other evidence, including other people's experience, not just your own.

Scientific Experiments

I'm going to adopt a fairly narrow definition of "science" here. By "science," I mean well-controlled scientific experiments, published in peer reviewed journals, then replicated by others. To be sure, "science," broadly conceived, includes much more than just controlled experiments.   It includes careful observation of phenomena. It includes an attempt to theorize about and rule out various alternative explanations for the phenomena. It includes qualitative research, not just quantitative measurement. A good portion of the afterlife literature is "scientific" in that broader sense. But most people, when they say "science," are thinking of carefully controlled experiments, published in scientific journals, then replicated.

When we use "science" in that narrower sense, we find very little of it on questions of the afterlife. There are a few relevant controlled trials, published in peer-reviewed journals, but not many.   There are many reasons for the lack of such research. Science is a method suited for exploration of the material, physical world. It is not well-suited for testing propositions about a non-material, non-physical dimension. In addition, the events we are talking about – NDEs, mediumship, ADCs, etc. – are not things that submit to experimental control in the laboratory, nor to mechanical replication. They are unique events that happen in unpredictable ways, at unpredictable times. I mentioned other reasons for lack of such research in the Introduction – lack of funding, negative stigma within the scientific establishment, risk to reputation and career damage, challenges to experimental design, and ethical problems.

For all these reasons, science in narrow sense is lacking, when it comes to the afterlife. That is much more true when we consider the question of *animal* afterlife. I managed to scrounge up one controlled study, and to be honest, I was surprised to find that much. No one (or almost no one) is doing controlled scientific research on animal afterlife. We're barely doing any on an afterlife for humans; forget animals.

That is the main downside of taking the scientific approach to this question. If you are looking for randomized, controlled experiments on animal afterlife, there is almost nothing to go on. If you want to assess the evidence, you will need to find another way to do it. If you are waiting for Science to give you the answer, don't hold your breath; you're going to be waiting a long time. You will find out the answer for yourself long before the scientists do.

––––––––––

Courtroom Standard

Many veterans in the afterlife literature understand this, and they suggest we use a courtroom model to approach this evidence instead. They think that a courtroom standard is a much better fit for the situation. For instance, Michael Tymn, a prominent afterlife historian, said that evidence for an afterlife "falls much more in the area of courtroom science than laboratory science."

Another afterlife researcher, Victor Zammit, himself a lawyer, echoed this idea – that afterlife questions are best addressed not by waiting for a long series of controlled laboratory experiments to decide the question, but by using the same standards courts use every day to decide important cases.

Courtroom judgement relies on reason and argument. It often relies on eye-witness testimony. Experts are often called to testify about particular topics or to give their opinion. Courtrooms use other forms of evidence as well. All of this – expert testimony, eye-witness reports, and reasoned argument – is present in the afterlife literature.

There is a difference, of course. No one is testifying under oath here. No one is being cross-examined by a hostile attorney trying to shred their credibility. This isn't an actual courtroom. We are just using an analogy.

If you adopt the courtroom standard, you are looking at the evidence, trying to be impartial, and using your judgment. You are using one of two criteria to make the decision:

1. **Preponderance of the Evidence.** In what direction does the *majority* of the evidence point? This is the criteria used to decide most civil cases, "preponderance of the evidence." If 60% of the evidence points towards animal afterlife, and 40% points away from it, then most of the evidence – the preponderance of the evidence – supports animal afterlife. So you would choose the former.

2. Beyond a Reasonable Doubt. Does the evidence prove *beyond a reasonable doubt* that animals have an afterlife? This is the standard used in most criminal trials. Note, the standard is not beyond any "conceivable" doubt – any doubt that you might come up with – but beyond any *reasonable* doubt.

If you are using the courtroom standard, you can pick either of these criteria. Personally, I prefer "preponderance of the evidence," for several reasons. It fits the situation better. The "beyond a reasonable doubt" criteria is used in criminal cases, to weight the situation in the favor of the defendant, so as to avoid convicting an innocent person. Animal afterlife isn't accused of a crime, and we don't need to tilt the scales in one direction or another. No one is at risk of losing life and liberty here. We are just asking whether animals have an afterlife. I used the "preponderance of the evidence" standard for decades in my professional work, and I found it to be a straightforward, sensible way to approach cases. In addition, I think it is easy to come up with "reasonable doubts" about many of these cases, especially in our current materialistic culture, where skepticism and even cynicism about most of these phenomena are the default assumption. If you use the "reasonable doubt" criterion, you risk shutting down further consideration at the starting gate.

You are welcome to adopt the "beyond a reasonable doubt" standard if you like, though. Just remember that the standard is a *reasonable* doubt, not any doubt whatsoever. Skeptics are marvelously inventive in concocting scenarios to cast doubt on these reports. When one alternative explanation is knocked down, they come up with another. When the second explanation is refuted, they come up with a third. This can go on and on, through refutation of dozens of alternative explanations. At a certain point, this doubt is no longer "reasonable" anymore. It is a dogmatic insistence on doubt, based on commitment to a materialist worldview. We should be more open-minded than that, and follow the evidence where it leads.

The courtroom approach (preponderance of the evidence) has several advantages and disadvantages, which I'll review briefly. In terms of advantages, firstly, it is a reasonably good fit for the phenomena we are dealing with. It is a lot better fit than controlled, scientific studies under laboratory conditions, published in peer-reviewed journals, then replicated.

Second, it is a standard which is available. As I've mentioned, there are almost no controlled scientific experiments on animal afterlife, for many reasons. If we are waiting for Science to answer this question, we are going to be waiting an awfully long time. In the absence of randomized controlled scientific experiments demonstrating animal afterlife, the courtroom standard is a workable alternative.

Third, the standards used in a courtroom are respected ones; they are neither flimsy nor unreasonable. Courtrooms use these standards thousands of times a day to make critically important decisions. If the standards are good enough for them, perhaps they are good enough for us.

The courtroom standard has several disadvantages as well. The first one I already mentioned – this is not an actual courtroom. There is no cross-examination of witnesses. There is no seasoned lawyer trying to undermine the witnesses' credibility or pull apart their stories. In a real courtroom, that setup would not fly; it would be a one-sided case.

That is pretty much the situation we have here: me, presenting a rather one-sided view of the evidence. I admit that is so. In my defense, I have put forth the most common skeptical counter-explanations for the evidence (e.g., hallucination) – the ones you hear most often in the media – but, for reasons I mentioned in the Introduction, I have not attempted to adequately represent the hardcore skeptic/materialist "side" of the argument. I did not try to play opposing counsel and tear down the credibility of the witnesses.

I did not leave the hardcore materialist/skeptic side entirely unrepresented. I did discuss the most popular counter-arguments. However, I did not try to aggressively pick apart every story, nor did I try to imagine every possible counter-explanation for every report. For the reasons I mentioned earlier, I am simply not interested in doing that. If I did, it would be a very long and different book, and one I would not want to write. For the most part, I am just letting people tell their own stories, and letting those stories speak for themselves.

I acknowledge that this is a disadvantage, at least as far as this book goes. If you would like to hear more from hardcore skeptics, just search any of these topics, combined with terms like "skeptic" or "debunked." The skeptical side of the argument is easy enough to find, because their voices dominate most media. Wikipedia, for example, is heavily curated by materialist/skeptics trying to root out what they deride as "pseudo-science," so you can find their positions well-represented there. This is one reason I didn't fret too much about playing opposing counsel for the hardcore skeptic crowd. They are already the loudest, best represented voice in the conversation. But feel free to search for that information, if you want to hear more from that side of the issue.

The second disadvantage is that the courtroom approach relies on eyewitness testimony, and eyewitness testimony can be unreliable. Since we are basing so much of our "case" on eyewitness reports, we should be aware of this shortcoming.

There is a substantial psychological literature on this topic. In a nutshell, it shows that eye-witness testimony can be seriously mistaken.[1] That is not to say that *all* eyewitness testimony is unreliable, of course, just that it *can* be so, especially under certain conditions. For instance, if the eyewitness is prejudiced against the defendant based on race or gender, if the sighting is brief or under poor lighting, or if inappropriate police or investigative procedures are used, then the eyewitness report is likely to be unreliable. Other factors, such as stress and the fallibility of human memory, also enter into it.

I don't want to exaggerate the unreliability of eyewitness reports. Courts of law continue to use eyewitness testimony every day to help make huge decisions, and some academics argue that we have gone too far in impugning their reliability.[2] When you can rule out some of the factors I mentioned above, you can have more confidence in their testimony.

Specifically, if you can show that the witness was not prejudiced, did not have clear expectations of seeing something in particular, was not under severe stress, had reasonable exposure time, and that inappropriate police or investigative procedures were not used, then you can be more confident in their report. We have seen many DKD cases, in which there was no expectation of seeing what was seen. We have reviewed many cases where there was no emotional bond, many cases where the witness was relaxed, many cases involving long and repeated exposures. We have also had skeptics and non-believers as eyewitnesses. All of that adds to the reliability of these reports.

In addition, when you have multiple eye-witnesses, then you can feel much more confident in the reliability of their report. That is precisely why I included many multiple witness reports in the book. We have reviewed many reports where there were multiple eyewitnesses.

Nevertheless, we are relying heavily on eyewitness testimony, so we need to recognize that it can be unreliable at times.

The last factor I need to mention, which can either be an advantage or a disadvantage, is the way we make our decision. In the courtroom analogy, we are the judge. A judge is supposed to be impartial, deciding cases on their merits, not being influenced by his/her own feelings about the matter. If we use the courtroom analogy as a reminder of the need for objectivity and reason, then it can be an advantage. If we forget it, though, it becomes a disadvantage. If you are reading this book, you probably have feelings about this topic, and you probably would like things to come out in favor of animal afterlife. But as a judge, you can't let your personal feelings get in the way of your judgment. Judges are human, so this is more an ideal than a practical reality, but we should still strive to be objective and impartial in our judgments. We should try to make the decision based on reason, argument, and evidence, not based on our feelings.

———————

Intuition

The intuitive approach involves taking an overall look at the evidence, and then getting an intuitive "feel" for what you make of it. What does your "gut" or your "heart" tell you, after listening to the evidence and arguments? Do animals exist in an afterlife or not?

The advantage of this method is its simplicity. It doesn't take extended thought or analysis. You just consult your intuitive sense of it. Some people place a lot of trust in their intuition, and they find this approach very natural. At times, your intuitive "read" of a situation can be more rapid and accurate than a careful, rational analysis.

The disadvantage of using intuition is that it can be wrong sometimes. Some people find it difficult to separate intuition from emotion, and emotion-driven reasoning can be unreliable.

Personally, I am too much of a left-brain, analytical thinker to rely solely on intuition. I respect my intuition, but, given how I am put together, I don't want to entrust a question like this to intuition alone. I have to use reason and analysis, too. That's just how I am. But you may be different.

––––––––––

Estimating Cumulative Probability

Speaking of being a left-brain, analytical type, this approach will appeal to people who like numbers. It involves estimating cumulative probabilities – specifically, the probability that *all the evidence is invalid*. We frame the issue that way – "all the evidence is invalid" -- because, if that is so, then there is no animal afterlife. However, if it is not so – if all the evidence is not invalid; if one part is valid – then animals have an afterlife.

So the question is this: "What is the probability that all the evidence before us is invalid?" In this context, "valid" means that the case provides genuine evidence of animal afterlife. "Invalid" means the opposite – the case is not genuine evidence of afterlife but instead the result of fraud, misperception, hallucination, or the like.

If you recall, the white crow principle says that we don't need *all* of the cases to be valid; we just need *one* of them to be. That is enough to demonstrate that animals – at least one of them, anyway – exist in an afterlife of some sort.

You may be wondering, "How the heck are we supposed to know which cases are valid and which cases are not?" Good question. There is no way to know for sure. There is no way to figure out what the "real" probability is. When you're flipping a coin, you know you've got a 50% chance of getting heads, and a 50% chance of getting tails.

Straightforward enough. But we're dealing with the afterlife here. When it comes to the afterlife, we can't know what the true, objective probabilities are that these cases are valid or invalid. To know that objectively, you would need either access to the afterlife or certainty of its nonexistence. If we had either of those, I wouldn't be writing this book, and you wouldn't be reading it.

So, in the absence of omniscience, we are left to our own judgment. We can estimate the probabilities, using subjective judgment. There is nothing wrong with that. We use subjective judgment all day, every day. Without it, we would be non-functional lumps of dough, sitting in the corner, not knowing what to do next.

However, we need to recognize the limitations of subjective estimates. Our estimates do not represent the "real" probability of animal afterlife – they only represent our subjective estimate of that probability. This will be more a problem for some than others.

Some people trust their judgment, and some don't. This approach will appeal to the former more than the latter.

If you're not a math person, don't be intimidated. The calculation is very simple. It works like this. Normally, we talk about probability as the chance of one event happening. What is the chance of flipping tails, for instance? It's 50%. *Cumulative* probability is the chance that several events happen, not just one. For example, what is the chance of flipping three tails consecutively? It's 12.5%. To get the cumulative probability, you multiply the individual probabilities together: 0.5 x. 0.5 x 0.5 = 0.125.

Let's return to our question, "What is the cumulative probability that all of these cases are invalid?" We have framed the question in terms of invalidity, because of the white crow principle. We just need one white crow. If all the cases are invalid, then all the crows are indeed black; there are no white crows. So that's the question – are *all* the cases black crows?

If we wanted to really give ourselves a headache, we could estimate the probability of each case being invalid. There are thousands of cases, though, so let's not do that. I like numbers, but I don't like them *that* much.

To make the question manageable, we will break the evidence into areas – NDEs, ADCs, etc. – and consider those areas one at a time. That is a simpler and more conservative approach.

To answer the question ("what is the cumulative probability that the evidence in all of these areas is invalid?"), we estimate the probability that the evidence in each area is invalid. Then we multiply those probabilities together. [3]

If you would like to try this approach, look at each of the areas listed below. Get out a note pad. For each area, ask yourself, *"What do I think the probability is, that all the evidence in this area is invalid (or that none of it is valid – same thing; none of it gives any genuine evidence of animal afterlife)?*

Then take the individual figures and multiply them together. The result is the probability that all of the evidence is invalid.

I'll illustrate. For each area listed below, I have provided an estimate for the chance that all the evidence in that area is invalid. I chose what I consider to be conservative estimates. My own estimates are much lower, but I am biased, and I don't want my numbers to skew yours. If you are very skeptical, you might set the percentages even higher. I'm just trying to illustrate the process.

- o NDEs: 60% (i.e., there is a 60% chance that all of the NDE evidence for animal afterlife is invalid; not one account provides valid evidence)

- o ADCs: 40% (40% chance that all ADC evidence for animal afterlife is invalid; not one account is valid)

- o DBVs: 70%

- o Ghost reports: 90%

- o Mediumship: 50%

- o Physical mediumship: 90%

- o EVP: 90%

- o OBEs: 95%

- o Spirit photography: 85%

If you multiply all of those fractions together, you get a combined probability of 5%. Based on your subjective judgement, there is a 5% chance that the evidence in all areas is invalid – a 5% chance of there being no white crows. To flip it around, your assessment of the evidence suggests that there is a 95% chance of animal afterlife – a 95% chance that at least one white crow is flying around in there somewhere.

The balance of probabilities, then, suggests that, based on your judgment, it is much more likely that animals have an afterlife than not.

There are some advantages to this approach, and some disadvantages. The advantages are that it helps you to be more precise about your judgment of the evidence, rather than think in broad, general terms. It also illustrates the power of cumulative probability. Even if you have a fairly high degree of skepticism about many of these areas (as in the example above), the cumulative probability that there are no white crows can come out surprisingly low.

I mentioned the main disadvantage earlier. These are subjective judgments, not objective assessments. There is no way to know the "real" probability of animal afterlife, so these numbers represent your subjective assessment of that probability. Nothing wrong with using subjective estimates; we just need to remember that is what we are doing.

We shouldn't get carried away with the numbers, either. It's best to consider this a rough, back-of-the-napkin estimate, not a precise figure.

_____

Best Explanation

The final approach, which I think is a very good one, involves asking yourself, "What is the best explanation for the evidence before us?"

Broadly speaking, there are two potential explanations for the evidence:

1. The evidence suggests that, after physical death, the soul/personality of animals continue to exist in some type of afterlife.

2. The evidence only reflects normal, physical causes; it has nothing to do with an alleged afterlife.

With respect to the second option, I have discussed some of the most popular skeptical counter-explanations throughout the book – hallucination, fraud, misperception, imaginative fantasy, etc. I have also reviewed many cases that ran counter to those explanations.

In fact, the majority of the cases we reviewed had at least one feature that ran counter to those skeptical counter-explanations:

- DKD cases, in which the person did not realize the animal was dead at the time of the experience.

- Multiple witness accounts, in which several different people all reported seeing the same "deceased" animal at different times.

- Cases in which there was no emotional connection between the experiencer and the animals being seen.

- Appearances to skeptics, in which "deceased" animals appeared to people who disbelieved in the afterlife and/or animal afterlife.

- "Rescue" ADCs, in which the timing of the experience was critical in alerting a person to danger.

o   Shared NDEs and DBVs, in which a person at bedside
     has an experience paralleling that of the person dying.

What is the best explanation for this evidence? What is the most
likely or probable explanation? Is it that animals exist in an afterlife
of some sort, or is it that these cases are all the result of normal,
material processes, confined to this physical world?

   As I'm sure you know by now, I find it hard to dismiss the
evidence as merely grief-induced hallucinations, fraud,
misperception, and the like. In my view, those explanations just
don't hold water. More skeptical people, though, will see it
differently.   Many hardcore materialist skeptics prefer *any*
physical/material explanation, no matter how implausible, to
belief in an afterlife. I am not a materialist skeptic, though, so I
come to different conclusions.

   This approach has two big advantages. First, it is a very
straightforward and reasonable approach. You simply ask, what is
the best explanation for the evidence?

   Second, it is a standard that is routinely used in both
science and philosophy. It is often referred to as "inference to the
best explanation."

   Third, it helps us from getting stuck in unproductive
arguments about whether something is "proven" or not. Proof
rarely exists, either in philosophy or science. What we have instead
are various explanations with different amounts of evidence in

their favor. It is not a matter of "proof." It is a matter of deciding which explanation is the best – which has the most support, which is the simplest, which has the most explanatory power.

To think in terms of "best explanation" rescues us from arrogant assertions about "proof." I am not claiming "proof" of anything. I have presented evidence. I leave it to you to decide what you think the best explanation for that evidence is.

As far as disadvantages, we might choose a preferred explanation, rather than the best one. We all bring biases and preferences to the table, and these can influence judgment. It doesn't matter whether you're a believer or a skeptic; we all have biases. Hardened skeptics sometimes condescend to believers and pride themselves on judging things "objectively," but skeptics can be just as biased as believers.

The second disadvantage is that deciding what the "best explanation" is depends on your knowledge base; it depends on how well you know the evidence. If you have big gaps in your knowledge, then you will be handicapped in your ability to determine the best explanation. Unfortunately, most people, especially those who are relatively new to an area, overestimate their knowledge and do so with utter confidence. The name for this is the Dunning-Kruger effect. I encourage you to look it up, if you don't know about it. It's an explanation of why ignorant people are often very confident in their opinion. They don't know enough to know how much they don't know. Don't be one of those people. Make sure you have the knowledge necessary to make an informed judgment. Otherwise, just suspend judgment and keep learning.

That is part of why I wrote the book, in fact. I wanted to inform people about the evidence, so they could make an informed judgment. Most people are unaware of most of what I have discussed in this book. For the same reason, I have repeatedly emphasized that it helps to understand the general literature on these topics. That is where you will find most of the evidence for the phenomena we are discussing. Animal reports are just a tiny sliver of that.

If you have an informed opinion, though, using "best explanation" is a good approach.

————

Your Decision

So, we have reviewed the evidence and six approaches to it.

Which of the approaches do you prefer? Personally, I use a combination of "best explanation," the courtroom standard (preponderance of the evidence), and personal experience. I like playing with cumulative probability, too, mostly for fun. I would add controlled scientific experiments, but there isn't enough to throw in the stew.

That's me, though. You may prefer different approaches. I encourage you to be conscious about the standard(s) you are using to decide, rather than just winging it. I also encourage you to use several approaches in combination, rather than just one. Heck, use all six if you like.

So, I leave the decision to you. When you consider the evidence and arguments, do you believe that animals have an afterlife? Do their spirits continue to exist after their bodies die, or is that the end of the story?

Chapter 17

Afterword

I could have gone beyond the question of whether animals have an afterlife and tried to tackle other questions. For instance, I could have tried to address any of the following issues:

- o If animals have an afterlife, what sort of afterlife is it? What do they do all day? Do they mix with human beings? Are they still a part of our lives, or do they hang out with their own species?

- o Can "departed" animals communicate with us? And we with them? If so, how?

- o Do animals reincarnate? If so, do human beings ever get reborn as animals, or vice versa?

- o How do animals interact on the other side? Is it all peace, love, and harmony, or is there some type of competition or aggression between them? Do they ever harm or kill each other? What about hunting and fishing?

Those are interesting questions, and you can find people who have opinions on them. However, I did not want to tackle them here.

I wanted to keep the focus on the more basic, fundamental question of whether animals have an afterlife at all. Because, if they don't, all those other questions are irrelevant. Besides, the question of afterlife is the one most animal lovers struggle with, when their pet dies. Also, it is a lot harder to find *evidence* on the questions above. You can find plenty of opinions, and some level of consensus among those opinions, but you can't find a whole lot of clear evidence.

Personally, I don't worry too much about the questions above. As long as I know animals have an afterlife, that's the main thing; that's good enough for me. I trust God and his staff to work out the details.

––––––––––

I hope you found the book interesting or helpful. If you'd like to drop me a line, I can be reached at edanderson8@comcast.net.

Thanks for reading. I wish you and your animal friends well.

Notes

Chapter 2: Overview of the Evidence

1. *Dogs That Know When Their Owners Are Coming Home*, Rupert Sheldrake.
2. *Psychic Pets*, Emma Heathcote-Jones
3. *Resurrecting Leonora Piper: How Science Discovered the Afterlife*, by Michael Tymn

Chapter 3: Near-Death Experiences

1. Some suggestions, if you would like to explore this area further: *Heading Towards Omega*, by Kenneth Ring, PhD; *Evidence of the Afterlife*, by Jeffrey Long, MD; *Consciousness Beyond Life*, by Pim von Lommel, MD; or *After*, by Bruce Greyson, MD.

2. Scott Smith, *The Soul of Your Pet*

3. Sources included Kim Sheridan, Animals and the Afterlife; Niki Shanahan, *The Rainbow Bridge*; Scott Smith, *The Soul of Your Pet; neardeath.com, and NDE Experiences with Pets Facebook page*

4. Nderf.org, case #6037, cited on the NDE Experiences with Pets Facebook page

5. Scott Smith, *The Soul of Your Pet*

6. Kim Sheridan, *Animals and the Afterlife*

7. Dr. Raymond Moody compiled some shared NDEs in *Glimpses of Eternity*.

8. Niki Behrikis Shanahan, *The Rainbow Bridge*.

9. See, for example, *Lessons from the Light*, by Kenneth Ring, or *Transformed by the Light*, by Cherie Sutherland.

10. Kim Sheridan, *Animals and the Afterlife*

Chapter 4: Visual After-Death Communications

1. Bill and Judy Guggenheim, *Hello from Heaven*. Despite the cheesy title, the Guggenheims researched this area for years and compiled a wealth of information about it.

2. For example, Emma Heathcote-Jones, *After-Death Communication*; see also adcrf.org.

3. Sources included Kim Sheridan, *Animals and the Afterlife*; Vincent and Margaret Gaddis, *The Strange World of Animals and Pets*; Slyvia Barbanell, *When Your Animal Dies*; Scott Smith, *The Soul of Your Pet*; Bill Schul, *Animal Immortality*; Harold Sharp, *Animals in the Spirit World*; Fate Magazine, 1996, *Psychic Pets and Spirit Animals*; and David Fontana, *Is There an Afterlife?*

4. Juliaassante.com/blog

5. Kim Sheridan, *Animals and the Afterlife*

6. Scott Smith, *The Soul of Your Pet*

7. Vincent and Margaret Gaddis, *The Strange World of Animals and Pets*
8. Slyvia Barbanell, *When Your Animal Dies*
9. Vincent and Margaret Gaddis, *The Strange World of Animals and Pets*
10. Scott Smith, *The Soul of Your Pet*
11. Bill Schul, *Animal Immortality*
12. Steve Volk, *Fringeology*
13. Kim Sheridan, *Animals and the Afterlife*
14. Scott Smith, *The Soul of Your Pet*
15. Bill and Judy Guggenheim, *Hello from Heaven*, chapter 13

Chapter 5: Do Animals Qualify for the Afterlife?

1. *Views on the Afterlife*, Pew Research poll, 2021. The US is a more religious country than most. Global data show the split is more like 50/50 worldwide.
2. IPSOS Global @dvisory: Supreme Being(s), the Afterlife, and Evolution.
3. *Do All Dogs Go to Heaven,* by Kenneth Royal, April Kedrowicz, and Amy Synder of North Carolina State University College of Veterinary Medicine, 2016.
4. *The Emotional Lives of Animals*, by Marc Bekoff
5. *Are We Smart Enough to Know How Smart Animals Are*, Frans de Waal
6. *Wild Justice: The Moral Lives of Animals*, by Marc Bekoff and Jessica Pierce.

7. J. Decety and J. Cowell, *The Complex Relation between Morality and Empathy*, Trends in Cognitive Science, July 2014

8. *Wild Justice: The Moral Lives of Animals*, by Marc Bekoff and Jessica Pierce.

9. ibid

Chapter 6: Auditory, Tactile, and Olfactory ADCs

1. Kim Sheridan, *Animals and the Afterlife*

2. Scott Smith, *The Soul of Your Pet*

3. Kim Sheridan, *Animals and the Afterlife*

4. Scott Smith, *The Soul of Your Pet*

5. Sources include Kim Sheridan, *Animals and the Afterlife*; Scott Smith, *The Soul of Your Pet*; Bill Schul, *Animal Immortality*; Elliot O'Donnell, *Animal Ghosts*; Sylvia Barbanell, *When Your Animal Dies*, Fate Magazine; Harold Sharp, Animals in the Spirit World; and Vincent and Margaret Gaddis, *The Strange World of Animals and Pets*

6. Bill Schul, *Animal Immortality*

7. Fate Magazine, *Psychic Pets and Spirit Animals*

Chapter 7: Mediumship

1. Overviews of the literature on mediumship can be found in Chris Carter, *Science and the Afterlife Experience* (see Part III); Victor Zammit, A Lawyer Presents Evidence for the Afterlife; David Fontana, *Is There an Afterlife?*; and Michael

Tymn, Afterlife Explorers (early history). There are many other sources, but those will get you started.

2. Kim Sheridan, *Animals and the Afterlife*
3. Slyvia Barbanell, *When Your Animal Dies*
4. Kim Sheridan, *Animals and the Afterlife*
5. Elena Mannes, *Soul Dog*
6. Harold Sharp, *Animals in the Spirit World*
7. Karen Anderson, *The Amazing Afterlife of Animals*
8. For example, Jessica Utts and Brian Josephson, *The Paranormal: The Evidence and Its Implications for Consciousness*, 1996; or Daryl Bem and Charles Honorton, *Does Psi Exist? Replicable Evidence for an Anomalous Process of Information Transfer*, Psychological Bulletin, vol. 115, 1994
9. *Death, Dying and Shifting Paradigms: An Interview with Julia Assante.* Edge Magazine, 2014.
10. Rock, A. J., Beischel, J., & Cott, C. C. (2009). *Psi vs. survival: A qualitative investigation of mediums' phenomenology comparing psychic readings and ostensible communication with the deceased.* Transpersonal Psychology Review, 13, 76-89; Beischel, J., Rock, A., & Boccuzzi, M. (2013, June); and Beischel, J., Rock, A. J., & Boccuzzi, M. (under review). Somatic psi and survival psi: Quantitative phenomenological analyses of blinded mediums' experiences of psychic readings and communication with the deceased.
11. For more information about the telepathy question, see David Fontana's *Is There an Afterlife?* or Leslie Kean's *Surviving Death.*

12. See windbridge.org for an overview of this research; Dr. Gary Schwartz has also conducted controlled experiments on mediumship; see his book, *The Afterlife Experiments*, for details. Other

13. Beischel, J., 2012. *Anomalous information reception by credentialed mediums regarding non-human animal discarnates.* Publication in progress.

Chapter 8: Physical Mediumship

1. Leslieflint.com
2. Leslie Kean, *Surviving Death*
3. For good overviews of physical mediumship, see Leslie Kean, *Surviving Death;* Michael Tymn, *The Afterlife Explorers* (early history); David Fontana, *Is There an Afterlife?*; and Victor Zammit, *A Lawyer Presents the Evidence for the Afterlife*
4. Neville Randall, *Life After Death*
5. Harold Sharp, *Animals in the Spirit World*
6. Sylvia Barbanell, *When Your Animal Dies*

Chapter 9: The Blob: Group Souls for Animals?

1. Thomas Merton, *New Seeds of Contemplation*
2. David Fontana, *Is There an Afterlife?*

Chapter 10: Deathbed Visions

1. Christopher Kerr, MD, *Death is But a Dream*
2. For overviews of DBVs, see Christopher Kerr, *Death is But a Dream*; Carla Will-Brandon, One Last Hug Before I Go: *The Mystery and Meaning of Deathbed Visions*; or Peter Fenwick, *The Art of Dying*.
3. Christopher Kerr, MD, *Death is But a Dream*
4. Peter Fenwick, *The Art of Dying*
5. Niki Behrikis Shanahan, *The Rainbow Bridge*
6. Scott Smith, *The Soul of Your Pet*
7. Gary Rotstein, *Pittsburg Post-Gazette*
8. Dr. Vernon Neppe, *oberf.org, case #17*
9. Fate Magazine, *Psychic Pets and Spirit Animals*
10. Other sources besides those mentioned above included Arthur Myers, *Communicating With Animals*; Rob Gutro, *Pets and the Afterlife*; Stafford Betty, *When Did You Ever Become Less by Dying?*; and Margrit Coates, *Communicating with Animals*.

Chapter 11: Ghost Reports

1. For a few succinct overviews, see David Fontana, *Is There an Afterlife?*, Michael Schmicker, *Best Evidence*, or Chris Carter, *Science and the Afterlife Experience*. From there, you can follow the trail to more comprehensive source material, if you like.
2. Stafford Betty, *When Did You Ever Become Less by Dying?*

3. Anna Kambhampaty, *Many Americans Say They Believe in Ghosts. New York Times*, October 28, 2021.
4. Arthur Myers, *Communicating with Animals*
5. Elliot O'Donnell, *Animal Ghosts*
6. Scott Smith, *The Soul of Your Pet*
7. Other animal ghost reports can be found in Kim Sheridan, *Animals and the Afterlife*; Bill Schul, *Animal Immortality*; Elliot O'Donnell, *Animal Ghosts*; Scott Smith, *The Soul of Your Pet*; and Arthur Myers, *Communicating with Animals*.

Chapter 12: Out of Body Experience

1. *The Self Does Not Die*, by Titus Rivas, Anny Dirven, and Rudolf Smit.
2. *Mindsight,* by Dr. Kenneth Ring
3. For books covering evidentiary support for OBEs, see *The Self Does Not Die*, by Rivas et al; *Mindsight,* by Dr. Kenneth Ring; *Recollections of Death*, by Dr. Michael Sabom, *Leaving the Body*, by Scott Rogo; and *Consciousness Beyond the Body*, by Alexander DeFoe
4. Robert Monroe, *Ultimate Journey*
5. Harold Sharp, *Animals in the Spirit World*
6. Bill Schul, *Animal Immortality*
7. Emmanuel Swedenborg, *True Christianity*
8. Scott Smith, *The Soul of Your Pet*

Chapter 13: Instrumental Transcommunication

1. For a general overview of ITC, see David Fontana, *Is There an Afterlife?* The documentary, *Calling Earth*, provides some impressive examples.
2. For overviews of EVP, see Anabela Cardoso, *Electronic Voices,* or Tom and Lisa Butler, *There is No Death And There Are No Dead*
3. Tom and Lisa Butler, *There is No Death And There Are No Dead*
4. Ibid
5. Other examples of animal EVPs can be found in *There is No Death And There Are No Dead*, by Tom Butler, and *Recording Conversations with Spirits*, by Clive Steigner
6. https://rinaldigalleryimages.wordpress.com/
7. Vincent and Margaret Gaddis, *The Strange World of Animals and Pets*
8. Scott Smith, *The Soul of Your Pet*
9. Sylvia Barbanell, *When Your Animal Dies*
10. Ibid; also, Scott Smith, The Soul of Your Pet, and Harold Sharp, *Animals in the Spirit World*

Chapter 14: God's Character

1. Hugh Ross, *The Creator and the Cosmos*

Chapter 16: Weighing the Evidence

1. The seminal work here was Elizabeth Loftus, *Eyewitness Testimony.* Much debate and discussion followed.
2. John Wixted, et al. (2018). *Rethinking the Reliability of Eye-Witness Testimony.* Perspectives on Psychological Science, vol 13, issue 3.
3. Stafford Betty, *When Did You Ever Become Less by Dying?*

Bibliography

Anderson, Karen. *Hear All Creatures*. 2008, New River Press.

Anderson, Karen. *The Amazing Afterlife of Animals*. 2017, Painted Rain Publishing.

Barbanell, Sylvia. *When Your Animal Dies*. 1940, Spiritualist Truth Foundation.

Beischel, Julie. *Among Mediums: A Scientist's Quest for Answers*. 2013, Windbridge Institute. Also see Windbridge.org for summaries of the research.

Beischel, J., 2012. *Anomalous information reception by credentialed mediums regarding non-human animal discarnates*. Presented the study at the 31st Annual Meeting of the Society for Scientific Exploration in 2012

Bekoff, Marc. *The Emotional Lives of Animals*. 2007, New World Library.

Bekoff, Marc & Pierce, Jessica. *Wild Justice: The Moral Lives of Animals*. 2009, University of Chicago Press.

Betty, Stafford. *When Did You Ever Become Less by Dying? Afterlife: The Evidence*. 2016, White Crow Books.

Butler, Tom and Lisa. *There is no Death and There are no Dead*. 2019, AA-EVP Publishing.

Carter, Chris. *Science and the Afterlife Experience: Evidence for the Immortality of Consciousness.* 2012, Inner Traditions.

Coates, Margrit. *Communicating with Animals.* 2012, Random House.

De Foe, Alexander. *Consciousness Beyond the Body: Evidence and Reflections.* 2016.

De Wall, Frans. *Are We Smart Enough to Know How Smart Animals Are?* 2016, Norton.

Fate Magazine. *Psychic Pets and Spirit Animals.* 1996, Gramercy.

Fenwick, Peter and Elizabeth. *The Art of Dying.* 2008, Continuum.

Fontana, David. *Is There an Afterlife? A Comprehensive Overview of the Evidence.* 2005, O Books.

Gaddis, Vincent and Margaret. *The Strange World of Animals and Pets.* 1970, Cowles Book Company.

Gurney, Carol. *The Language of Animals.* 2001, Bantam-Dell Publishing.

Gutro, Rob. *Pets and the Afterlife.* 2014.

Jones-Hunt, Jackie. *Proof Animals Have Souls.* 2014. House of Light Publishers.

Kerr, Christopher. *Death is But a Dream: Finding Hope and Meaning at Life's End.* 2020, Penguin Random House.

Long, Jeffrey and Perry, Paul. *Evidence of the Afterlife: The Science of Near-Death Experiences.* 2010, Harper Collins.

Kean, Leslie. *Surviving Death: A Journalist Investigates Evidence for an Afterlife*. 2017, Crown Archetype.

Kinnis, Hans. Itc-experiments.nl

Mannes, Elena. *Soul Dog*. 2014, Bear and Company.

Marks, Jeffrey A. *The Afterlife Interviews*. 2014, Arago Press.

Monroe, Robert. *Ultimate Journey*. 1994, Doubleday.

Myers, Arthur. *Communicating with Animals*. 1997, Contemporary Books.

Northrop, Suzanne. *Everything Happens for a Reason*. 2002, Jodere Group.

O'Donnell, Elliott. *Animal Ghosts*. 2012, Centennial edition, revised and updated by John E.L. Tenney.

Pitstick, Mark. *Soul Proof: Compelling Evidence that Life Continues After Physical Death*. 2016.

Randall, Neville. *Life After Death*. 1974, Robert Hale Publishing.

Rogo, D. Scott. *Leaving the Body*. 1983, Prentiss Hall.

Ring, Kenneth. *Mindsight*. 1999, William James Center for Consciousness Studies.

Ring, Kenneth. *Heading Toward Omega: In Search of the Meaning of the Near-Death Experience*. 1984, Quill.

Sabom, Michael. *Recollections of Death: A Medical Investigation*. 1981, Harper Collins.

Sartori, Penny. *The Wisdom of Near-Death Experiences*. 2014, Watkins Press.

Schmicker, Michael. *Best Evidence*. 2002, Writers Club Press.

Schul, Bill D. *Animal Immortality: Pets and their Afterlife*. 1990, Carol and Graf Publishers.

Schwartz, Gary E. *The Afterlife Experiments: Breakthrough Scientific Evidence of Life After Death*. 2002, Pocket Books.

Shanahan, Niki Behrikis. *The Rainbow Bridge: Pet Loss is Heaven's Gain*. 2007, Pete Publishing.

Sharp, Harold. *Animals in the Spirit World*. Originally published in 1996; revised edition 2018, Saturday Night Press Publications.

Sheridan, Kim. *Animals and the Afterlife*. 2003, Hay House.

Smith, Scott. *The Soul of Your Pet: Evidence for the Survival of Animals After Death*. 1998, Holmes Publishing Group.

Steigner, Clive. *Recording Conversations with Spirits*. 2019.

Swedenborg, Emmanuel. *True Christianity*. Originally published in 1771; new edition 2009, Swedenborg Foundation.

Tompkins, Ptolemy. *The Divine Life of Animals: One Man's Quest to Discover Whether the Souls of Animals Live On*. 2010, Three Rivers Press.

Varga, Josie. *A Call from Heaven*. 2017, Career Press.

Will-Brandon, Carla. *One Last Huge Before I Go: The Mystery and Meaning of Deathbed Visions*. 2000, Health Communications.

Zammit, Victor. *Afterlife Newsletter*, April 2014 edition.

Zammit, Victor and Wendy. *A Lawyer Presents the Evidence for the Afterlife.* 2013, White Crow Books.

Printed in Great Britain
by Amazon

38584169R00149